Loudoun County, Virginia

Order Book Abstracts

1761–1762

Ruth and Sam Sparacio

Heritage Books
2025

HERITAGE BOOKS

AN IMPRINT OF HERITAGE BOOKS, INC.

Books, CDs, and more—Worldwide

For our listing of thousands of titles see our website
at
www.HeritageBooks.com

Published 2025 by
HERITAGE BOOKS, INC.
Publishing Division
5810 Ruatan Street
Berwyn Heights, MD 20740

International Standard Book Number
Paperbound: 978-1-68034-590-2

LOUDOUN COUNTY, VIRGINIA
ORDERS
1757-1762

p.   - At a Court held for Loudoun Conty at the Courthouse on Tuesday the Ninth
449 day of June in the first year of the Reign of our Sovereign Lord George the Third
by the grace of God of Great Britain France and Ireland, King, Defender of the
faith, &c., Anno Domini one thousand seven hundred and sixty one, Before his
Majesty's Justices of the Peace for the said County, to wit;
FIELDING TURNER   GEORGE WEST   and
JAMES HAMILTON   JOHN MUCKLEHANEY, Gent;

- Surry, a Negro boy, and Celana, a Negro girl belonging to CHARLES BINNS
are adjudged by the Court, Surry to be twelve years and Celana to then years of age
- Indentures of Lease and Release between MAHLON JANNEY and SARAH
his Wife of the one part and AMOS GOODEN of the other part, were acknowledged by
the said MAHLON and SARAH, she having been first privily examined as the Law
directs, and the Receipt thereon endorsed was acknowledged by the said MAHLON
and together with the said Indentures of Lease and Release ordered to be recorded
- CHARLES TYLER, Gentl, a Justice named in the Commission of the Peace
for this County took the usual Oaths to his Majesty's Person and Government and
took and subscribed the Abjuration Oath and subscribed the Test and also took the
Oath of a Justice of the Peace and of the County Court in Chancery
        - Present CHARLES TYLER, Gent.
- Ordered that JEREMIAH HUTCHISON be appointed Surveyor of the Road
in the room of JOHN HUTCHISON, who is discharged from that Office
        - Present. FRANCIS PEYTON, Gent.
- BENJAMIN GRAYSON, Gent., a Justice of the Peace for this County took
the usual Oaths to his Majesty's Person and Government and took and subscribed
the Abjuration Oath and subscribed the Test, and also took the Oath of a Justice of
the Peace and of the County Court in Chancery
        - Present BENJAMIN GRAYSON, Gent.

p.   Loudoun County Court 9th of June 1761
450 - Ordered that FIELDING TURNER, JAMES HAMILTON, WILLIAM
     WEST, RICHARD COLEMAN, CHARLES TYLER, JOSIAS CLAPHAM,
FRANCIS PEYTON, JOHN MUCKLEHANEY and JAMES LANE, Gentlemen take
the List of Tithables for this County this present year
- Ordered that RICHARD COLEMAN, Gent., allot the hands to work on the
Road of which GREENBURY DORSEY is Surveyor
- Ordered that JAMES WILLIAMSON, JACOB MORRIS, RICHARD
PILES, JOHN PILES, JOHN PRICE and the hands of GEORGE WEST, Gent., do
work on the Road whereof said GEORGE WEST is Surveyor
- Ordered that GEORGE WEST, Gent., allot the hands to work on the Roads
whereof JOHN PEAKE and GEORGE TAYLOR are Overseers
- Indentures of Lease and Release between THOMAS JOHN of the one part
and JOHN HANBY of the other part and the Receipt thereon endorsed were acknow-

ledged by said THOMAS JOHN and ordered to be recorded
        - Ordered that JOHN PEAKE, ANDREW ADAM and GEORGE WEST,
JUNR. or any two thereof being first sworn before a Justice of this County do view
the most convenient way for a Road from MORRIS's FORD to the Road that leads to
DAWSON's FORD and make report of the conveniency and inconveniency thereof to
the Court
        - Ordered that STURMAN CHILTON be appointed Surveyor of the Highwaies
in the room of THOMAS LEWIS, who is discharged from that Office
        - An Indenture of Feofment between SAMUEL GRIGSBY of the one part and
JAMES LANE, JUNR. of the other part and the Receipt & Memorandum of Livery of
Seisen thereunder written were proved by the Oaths of BURKETT JETT and THO-
MAS CONNELL, witnesses thereto
        - The Last Will and Testament of HENRY INSLE, deced., was proved accor-
ding to Law by the Oath of WILLIAM ROSS, and by the Affirmations of WILLIAM
MEAD and JACOB WILDMAN (Quakers) witnesses thereto, and ordered to be re-
corded; And on the motion of MARY INSLE, the Executrix therein named, who made
Oath according to Law, Certificate is granted her for obtaining a Probat theref in due
form giving security, Whereupon she together with HUGH WEST and JOHN MOSS
her Securities, entered into and acknowedged Bond in the Penalty of five hundred
pounds with condition as the Law directs; And the said MARY INSLE, Widow of the
Testator, personally in Court renounced all benefit which she might claim by the said
Will

p.   Loudoun County Court 9th of June 1761
451   - Ordered that NICHOLAS MINOR, Gent., WILLIAM MEAD, WILLIAM
        ROSS and BENJAMIN EDWARDS, or any three of them, being first sworn
before a Justice of this County, do appraise in current money the slaves (if any) and
personal Estate of HENRY INSLE, deced., and return the Appraisment to the Court
        - The Last Will and Testament of GABRIEL ADAMS, deced., was proved ac-
cording to Law by the Oaths of WILLIAM STARKS and WILLIAM LITTLETON,
witnesses thereto, and ordered to be recorded; And on motion of WILLIAM ADAMS,
the Executor therein named, who made Oath according to Law, Certificate is granted
im for obtaining a Probat thereof in due form giving security; Whereupon he together
with JOHN MOSS and THOMAS LEWIS, his Securities, entered into and acknowledged their Bond in the Penalty of two hundred and fifty pounds current money with
conditions as the Law directs
        - Ordered that RICHARD COLEMAN, Gent., WILLIAM STARKS, WILLIAM
LITTLETON and JAMES COLEMAN, or any three thereof, being first sworn before
a Justice of this County, do appraise in current money the slaves (if any) and personal Estate of GABRIEL ADAMS, deced., and return the Appraisment to the Court
        - Indentures of Lease and Release between JONAS POTTS of the one part
and JAMES THOMAS of the other part and the Receipt thereon endorsed were acknowledged by the said JONAS, and MARY, the Wife of said JONAS, being first privily
examined relinquished here in Court her Right of Dower to the lands and premises
conveyed by the said Indenture, which are ordered to be recorded
        - The Last Will and Testament of JOSEPH McGEACH, deced., was proved
according to Law by the Oaths of JOHN McILHANEY, Gent., and by the Affirmation

of JOSEPH YATES (a Quaker) witnesses thereto, and ordered to be recorded; And on the motion of MARY McGEACH, the Executrix therein named, who made Oath according to Law, Certificate is granted her for obtaining a Probat thereof in due form giving security; Whereupon she together with NICHOLAS MINOR, her Security, entered into and acknowledged their Bond in the Penalty of five hundred pounds with condition as the Law directs

     - Ordered that GEORGE GREGG, FRANCIS ELGIN, JOSEPH CALDWELL and WILLIAM GOSSETT, or any three of them, being first sworn before a Justice of this county, do appraise in current money the slaves (if any) and personal Estate of JOSEPH McGEACH, deced, and return the Appraisment to the Court

     - A Report of the persons appointed to view the most convenient way for a Road from WILLIAM KIRK's Mill to LEESBURGH was returned in these words, vizt. "Whereas there was an Order issued from this Court some time ago directed to us the Subscribers requiring us to view and report the best way for a Road to be got from WILLIAM KIRK's Mill to this place, we being well acquainted with the situation of the lands, recommend that a Road be brought along by RALPH

p.   <u>Loudoun County Court 9th of June 1761</u>
452   BRADDOCK's thence to RICHARD ROBERTS's with a streight course to a
       Bridge in the Main Road nigh ROBERT POPKINS's Fence (above POPKINS's Plantation), June 9th 1761. JOSIAS CLAPHAM, JOHN TRAMMELL." Whereupon it is ordered that the same be cleared according to Law; that RICHARD ROBERTS be appointed Surveyor thereof, and that JOSIAS CLAPHAM, Gent., allot the hands to work thereon

     - WILLIAM ALLAN, Esqr., Plt. agt. BERNARD YOUNG, Deft.
     Upon an Attachment
  This day came Plt. by HUGH WEST, his Attorney, and Deft. came not altho' solemnly called, Therefore it is considered by the Court that Plt. recover against Deft. seventy pounds, five shillings and nine pence current money of Virginia with legal Interest thereon to be computed after the rate of five per centum per annum from the Eleventh day of December 1754 till payment and also his costs by him in this behalf expeded, and the Deft. in mercy, &c.

     - THOMAS LEWELLEN and JAMES JOHNS being further summoned as Garnishees in this suit, appeared and declared that they have in their hands of Deft.'s Effects forty eight pounds, five shillings and five pence current money of Virginia over and above what they formerly declared to have. It is therefore ordered that THOMAS LEWELLEN and JAMES JOHNS pay unto Plt. seventy eight pounds, five shillings and five pence current money of Virginia, it beiing the whole in their hands due upon a Bond from them, the said THOMAS LEWELLEN and JAMES JOHNS to the Deft.

     - Present JAMES LANE, Gent.
     - JOHN OSBORN an Evidence for WILLIAM ALLAN, Esqr., against BERNARD YOUNG, having attended Court two daies, ordered that the said WILLIAM ALLAN pay him fifty pounds of tobacco for the same
     - On motion of JOHN OSBORN his Ear mark is ordered to be recorded, vizt., a swallow fork and hole in the right Ear and a crop and hole in the left
     - On motion of WILLIAM ALLAN, his Ear mark is ordered to be recorded, vizt.

a swallow fork in the left Ear

    - On motion of JOHN TRAMMELL, his Ear mark is ordered to be recorded, vizt., a staple fork in each Ear

    - On motion of JOHN WILKS, his Ear mark is ordered to be recorded, vizt., a crop and underkeel in the left Ear, and a swallow fork in the right

    - A Deed of Poll or Gift from MOSES BOTTS to JOSHUA BOTTS was acknowledged by said MOSES and is ordered to be recorded

p.   Loudoun County Court 9th of June 1761
453   - Upon Petition of BENJAMIN SEBASTIAN against JAMES GOULDING for a Debt due by Account, This day came the parties by their Attornies and Deft. acknowledged Plt.'s demand for one pounds, ten shillings to be just. Therefoe it is considered by the Court that Plt. recover against Deft. the said one pound, ten shillings and his costs by him in this behalf expended

    - Ordered that JAMES HAMILTON, Gent., allot the hands to work on the Road whereof FRANCIS WILKS is Surveyor

    - Ordered that FRANCIS YELDALL, NICHOLAS OSBORN and JAMES CONNARD or any two thereof being first sworn before a Justice for this County, do view the most convenient way for a Road leading from POTOWMACK RIVER between the BLUE RIDGE and SHORT HILLs into the Road that leads to JOHN HOUGH's Mill and make report of the conveniency and inconveniency that will attend the same to the Court

    - Indentures of Lease and Release between JOSHUA GORE, JUNR., and ELIZABETH his Wife of the one part and JONATHAN CONARD of the other part and the Receipt thereon endorsed, were acknowledged by said JOSHUA and ELIZABETH, she having been first privily examined as the Law directs, and ordered to be recorded

    - Indentures of Lease and Release between JOSHUA GORE, JUNR. and ELIZABETH his Wife of the one part and NICHOLAS OSBORN, JUNR. of the other part and the Receipt thereon endorsed were acknowledged by the said JOSHUA and ELIZABETH, she having been first privily examined as the Law directs, and ordered to be recorded

    - Ordered that the Churchwardens of Cameron Parish bind out HENRY FRANKS, an Orphan of ten years and three months old, to THOMAS STUMP according to Law who is to learn him the Trade of a Cord Winder

    - Indentures of Lease and Release between JOSHUA GORE, JUNR. and ELIZABETH his Wife of the one part and GEORGE FOUT of the other part and the Receipt thereon endorsed were acknowleded by the said JOSHUA and ELIZABETH she having been first privily examined as the Law directs and ordered to be recorded

    - FRANCIS WILKS, Plt. against THOMAS GREGG, Exr. of JOHN GREGG, Deft.   Upon an Attachment
Continued till the next Court

    - Absent. GEORGE WEST, CHARLES TYLER,
                FRANCIS PEYTON & BENJAMIN GRAYSON, Gent.

    - RICHARD SNOWDEN, Plt. agt. DANIEL JAMES, Deft.   In Case
This day came as well Plt. by HUGH WEST, his Attorney, as Deft. in his proper

person, and Deft. acknowledged Plt.'s action for three pounds, fourteen shillings and five pence; Therefore with the assent of Plt., it is considered by the Court that Plt. recover against Deft. the said three pounds, fourteen shillings and five pence and his costs by him in this behalf expended, and the Deft. in mercy, &c.

- Upon Petition of ANTHONY RUSSELL and CHARLES BINNS setting forth that they are bound in this Court as securities for BENJAMIN GRAYSON, Gent., Guardian of WILLIAM GRAYSON, and that they conceive themselves to be in danger of suffering damages by reason of their being Securities as aforesaid; This day came as well the Petitiones as BENJAMIN GRAYSON who being fully heard, it is ordered that unless BENJAMIN GRAYSON give the Petitioners sufficient security to indemnify them against any damages that may happen to them by means of their being Securities as aforesaid, that then BENJAMIN GRAYSON deliver the Estate of WILLIAM GRAYSON into the hands of the Petitioners for their indemnity

- BENJAMIN GRAYSON, Gent. Guardian of WILLIAM GRAYSON, Infant, an Orphan of BENJAMIN GRAYSON, deced., returned an Account of the profits of the Orphan's Estate to which he made Oath and the same being examined and approved of by the Court is ordered to be recorded

- Ordered that JAMES HAMILTON and NICHOLAS MINOR, Gent., agree with workmen to repair the Prison built for this County

- JAMES GOLDING, Plt. agt. GEORGE HARDY, Deft. Upon an Attachmt. This day came Plt. by WILLIAM ELLZEY, his Attorney, and Deft. came not altho' solemnly called; Therefore it is considered by the Court that Plt. recover against Deft. one pound, nine shillings and six pence and also his costs by him in this behalf expended and the Deft in mercy &c.

- GEORGE VANIVIER, a Garnishee sworn declares that he has in his hands of the Deft.'s Estate one old Plough. CHARLES LEWIS, a Garnishee, being also sworn declares that he has in his hands of Deft.'s Estate and old Colter, an old Wheel, a Piggin, a Keeler and a Drawing Knife. Ordered that the said Garnishees deliver the goods to the Sherif and that he sell the same according to Law and render the money arising thereby to Plt. towards satisfying of his Judgment and costs aforesaid

- Ordered that FIELDING TURNER, Gent., allot the hands to work on the Road whereof ANTHONY RUSSELL, Gent., is Surveyor

p.   Loudoun County Court 9th of June 1761
455   - BENJAMIN GRAYSON, Gent., Plt. against JACOB MORRIS, Deft.
        In Case
This day came the parties by their Attornies and Deft. saving to himself all advantages of Exceptions as well to Plt.'s Writ as to his Declaration, prays and has leave to imparl till the next Court and then to plead

- Indentures of Lease and Release between JOHN GRANTAM of the one part and PHILIP NOLAND, Gent., of other part and the Receipt thereon endorsed were proved by the Oaths of NICHOLAS MINOR, Gent., HUGH WEST and WILLIAM BAKER, witnesses thereto, and ordered to be recorded

- An Indenture of Feofment beween PETER CRIGER of the one partand JAMES ABBETT of the other part and the Memorandum of Livery of Seisen thereon endorsed were proved by the Oaths of NICHOLAS MINOR Gent., JOHN MOSS, JUNR. and WLLIAM BAKER, witnesses thereto, and ordered to be recorded

- Ordered that the Court be adjourned till tomorrow morning eight o'clock
- The Minutes of these Proceedings were signed

                              "FIELDING TURNER"

- At a Court continued and held for Loudoun County at the Courthouse on
Wednesday the Tenth day of June one thousand seven hundred and sixty one,
Before his Majesty's Justices of the Peace for the said County, to wit;

FIELDING TURNER   AENEAS CAMPBELL   and
JAMES HAMILTON   JAMES LANE, Gent.   Gent.

- The Petition of ALEXANDER FARROW, Assignee of THOMAS MIDDLE-
TON the Third, against ISAAC PRESTON is discontinued
- Upon Petition of WILLIAM MARTHOS against JOHN DAVIS for a Debt
due by Note of Hand, This day came as well Plt. by HUGH WEST, his Attorney, as
Deft. in his proper person, who being fully heard, it is considered by the Court that Plt.
recover against deft. three pounds, three shillings and four pence and his costs by him
in this behalf expended, including seven shillings and six pence for a Lawyer's fee
- Upon Petition of WILLIAM BAYLIS against WILLIAM FIELDS for a Debt
due by Account, This day came as well Plt. by FRANCIS DADE, his Attorney, as
Deft. in his proper person

p.   Loudoun County Court 10th of June 1761
456   and Deft. acknowledged Plt.'s demand for four pounds, nine shillings and ten
        pence to be just; Therefore it is considered by the Court that Plt. recover
against Deft. the four pounds, nine shillings and ten pence and his costs by him in this
behalf expended, and Plt. agrees to stay the Execution of this Judgment till July
Court next
- Upon Petition of CHARLES BINNS against JOHN CAMBDEN for a Debt
due by Account, This day came Plt, and Deft. having been duly summoned was
solemnly called but came not. Therefore it is considered by the Court that Plt. recover against Deft. four pounds, sixteen shillings, his Debt due as aforesaid
- Upon Petition of JOHN MINOR and ELIZABETH his Wife under the age of
twenty one years by NICHOLAS MINOR the next Friend, against JOHN TRAM-
MELL for a Debt due by Account, This day came the parties by their Attornies who
being fully heard it is considered by the Court that Plts. recover against Deft. one
thousand pounds of crop tobacco, their Debt due as aforesaid, and their costs by them
in this behalf expended
- EZEKIEL HICKMAN an Evidence for JOHN MINOR and ELIZABETH his
Wife under the age of twenty one years by NICHOLAS MINOR their next Friend
against JOHN TRAMMELL, having attended Court six daies and for travelling thirty
miles from FREDERICK County and returning six times, ordered that said JOHN
and ELIZABETH pay him six hundred and ninety pounds of tobacco for the same
- The Petition of WILLIAM DODD against JOHN WORMSLEY is continued
till the next Court at motion and costs of Deft.
- The Petition of ROBERT SCOTT against PHILAMON CHESSIER is discontinued

      - The Petition of ROBERT SCOTT against JOSEPH DUNNAWAY is discontinued

      - Upon Petition of JOHN DAVIS against THOMAS KELLEY for a Debt due by Account, This day came as well Plt. in his proper person and Deft. by WILLIAM ELLZEY, his Attorney, who being fully heard, it is considered by the Court that the Petition be dismissed

      - A Deed of Gift from ANN MURPHEY to SARAH COLLINS and KEZIA COLLINS, Daughters of THOMAS COLLINS and WINIFRED his Wife, was proved by the Oaths of WILLIAM MURPHEY and BENJAMIN MASON, witnesses thereto, and is ordered to be recorded

      - Present.   JOSIAS CLAPHAM, Gent.

      - Prsent.   CHARLES TYLER, Gent.

p.   Loudoun County Court 10th of June 1761

457   - Absent. JAMES HAMILTON, Gent.

      - Messrs. NICHOLSON, STEPHENSON and COMPANY, Plts. agt. LEWIS ELLZEY, Deft.   In Debt

This day came the parties by their Attornies and Deft. acknowledged the action of the Plts. Therefore it is considered by the Court that Plts. recover against Deft. thirteen pounds, fifteen shillings and eight pence, the Debt in the Declaration mentioned, and their costs by them about their suit in this behalf expended and the Deft. in mercy &c., But this Judgment (the costs excepted) is to be discharged by paiment of six pounds, seventeen shillings and ten pence together with Interest for the same to be computed after the rate of five percentum per annum from the twelfth day of June 1745 to the time of paiment and one hundred and fifty nine pounds of tobacco and fifteen shillings

      - THOMAS AWBREY, Admr. of WALTER ENGLISH, deced., Plt. agt. WILLIAM SAUNDERS, Deft.   In Debt

This day came the parties by their Attornies and thereupon came also a Jury to wit

JOSHUA GORE	EZEKIEL HICKMAN	THOMAS OWSLEY
WILLIAM OWSLEY	BENJAMIN MASON	WILLIAM STEPHENS
NEWDIGATE OWSLEY	JOHN TRAMMELL	CHRISTOPHER PERFECT
WILLIAM ROSS	OWEN ROBERTS and	WILLIAM PEARL

who being elected tried and sworn the truth to speak upon the issue joined, upon their Oath do say that Deft. hath not paid to the Plt. fifteen hundred seventy eight pounds of tobacco and fifteen shillings the Debt in the Declaration mentioned in manner and form as Plt. against him hath complained, and they do assess the Plt.'s damages by occasion of the detention of the Debt to one pound of tobacco besides his costs; Therefore it is considered by the Court that Plt. recover against Deft. his Debt aforesaid together with the damages aforesaid in form aforesaid assessed and his costs by him about his suit in this behalf expended, and Deft. in mercy, &c.

      - The Petition of BENJAMIN GRAYSON and CRAVEN PEYTON against JOHN McMANAMY is discontinued being agreed, and it is ordered that Deft. pay unto Plts. their costs

      - Upon Petition of BENJAMIN GRAYSON and CRAVEN PEYTON against EDWARD HATTFIELD for a Debt due by Accounty, This day came Plts. by HUGH WEST their Attorney and Deft. being duly summoned and solemnly called came not; Therefore it is considered by the Court that Plts. recover against Deft. two pounds, five shillings and two pence, their Debt due as aforesaid, and their costs by them in this behalf expended

    - ThePetition of GEORGE SIMPSON against JOHN CAMBDEN is continued till next Court

    - The Petition of JOHN DAVIS against SAMPSON TURLEY, is continued till next Court

p.   <u>Loudoun County Court 10th of June 1761</u>

458   - Upon Petition of PATRICK RICE against SAMUEL HARRISS, JUNR., for a Debt due by a Note of Hand. This day came Plt. by HUGH WEST, his Attorney, and Deft. having been served with a copy of the Petition and summons was solemnly called but came not. Therefore it is considered by the Court that Plt. recover against Deft. one pound, nineteen shillings and eight pence and his costs by him in this behalf expended, including seven shillings and six pence for a Lawyer's fee

    - THOMAS BOTTS, Plt. agt. CHARLES CHINN, Deft.

    In Trespass Assault and Battery

This day came the parties by their Attornies (AARON BOTTS who became Security for Plt.'s costs in this suit is discharged) and EDWARD GARRETT comes into Court and undertakes for Plt. that in case Plt. shall be cast in this suit he shall pay and satisfy all such damages, costs and charges as shalal be awarded against him or that he will pay them for him; And thereupon came also a Jury to wit;

EZEKIEL HICKMAN	WILLIAM WOLLARD	JAMES ABBETT
BENJAMIN MASON	WILLIAM STEPHENS	WILLIAM ROSS
JOHN WINN	JOHN DAWSON	HUGH FOUCH
FRANCIS WILKS	EDWARD HARDEN and	THOMAS LEWIS

who being elected tried and sworn the truth to speak upon the issue joined, upon their Oath do say that Deft. is Guilty in manner and form as Plt. against him hath declared and they do assess Plt.'s damages by occasion thereof to twenty five shillings. Therefore it is considered by the Court that Plt. recover against Deft. his damages aforesaid in form aforesaid assessed and the Deft. may be taken, &c.

    - THOMAS BOTTS, Plt. agt. CHARLES CHINN, Deft. In Case

This day came the parties by their Attornies and thereupon came also a Jury to wit

EZEKIEL HICKMAN	WILLIAM WOLLARD	JAMES ABBETT
BENJAMIN MASON	WILLIAM STEPHENS	WILLIAM ROSS
JOHN WINN	JOHN DAWSON	HUGH FOUCH
FRANCIS WILKS	EDWARD HARDEN and	THOMAS LEWIS

who being elected tried and sworn the truth to speak upon the issue joined, upon their Oath do say that Deft. is Not Guilty as in pleading he hath alledged. Therefore it is considered by the Court that Plt. take nothing by his Bill but for his false clamour be in mercy, &c., and the Deft. go thereof without day and recover against Plt. his costs by him about his defence in this behalf expended

    - Present. JAMES HAMILTON, Gent.

    - NEWIDGATE OWSLEY, an Evidence for THOMAS BOTTS against CHARLES CHINN, having attended Court ten daies ordered that said THOMAS pay him two hundred and fifty pounds of tobacco for the same

p.   <u>Loudoun County Court 10th of June 1761</u>

459   - An Indenture of Feofment between JOHN COOK and ELIZABETH his Wife

of the one part and THOMAS CARTWRIGHT of the other part and the Memorandum of Livery of Seisen and Receipt endorsed were proved by the Oaths of AENEAS CAMPBELL, Gent., FRANCIS ELGIN and WILLIAM DODD, witnesses thereto, and together with a Commission for the acknowledgment and privy examination of said ELIZABETH, and the Certificate of the execution thereof are ordered to be recorded

- Upon the Proceedings taken and returned against JAMES KANNIDAY on Suspicion of his being Guilty of Stealing a Waistcoat and some stocking thread, the property of HENRY O'DANIEL, said JAMES appeared according to his Recognizance, whereupon it was demanded of him whether he was Guilty of the Felongy aforesaid or not, he said he was Not thereof Guilty. Thereupon HENRY O'DANIEL, MARY O'DANIEL and SARAH PONEL were sworn and examined as witnesses against said JAMES and he heard in his defence. On consideration whereof, it is the opinion of the Court that JAMES is Guilty of a Misdemeanor and it is ordered that he give Security for his good behavior for one year from this time, himself in ten pounds and two securities in five pounds each or to be committed to the Custody of the Sherif of this County there to remain until he finds such security

- HUGH BLACK, Plt. agt. LEVY LEWIS, Deft.   Upon an Attachment
Continued till the next Court

- JOHN OWSLEY, an Evidence for THOMAS BOTTS against CHARLES CHINN, having attended Court seven daies, ordered that said THOMAS pay him one hundred seventy five pounds of tobacco for the same

- SAMUEL SMITHERMAN, an Evidence for CHARLES CHINN at the suit of THOMAS BOTTS, having attended Court one day, ordered that said CHARLES pay him twenty five pounds of tobacco for the same

- THOMAS COLLINS, Plt. agt. THOMAS FIELDS, Deft.   In Case
This suit is dismissed, being agreed

- THOMAS HARRISON, JAMES NISBET, BENJAMIN GRAYSON and SPENCE GRAYSON, Executors of the Last Will and Testament of BENJAMAIN GRAYSON, Gent., deced., Plts. against THOMAS LEWELLING,. Deft.   In Case
Continued till next Court at motion and costs of Plts.

p.   Loudoun County Court 10th of June 1761
460   - PATRICK McKINZEY, Plt. against CHRISTOPHER PERFECT, Deft. In Case
This suit is dismissed, being agreed by the parties

- CHARLES CRYCROFT, Plt. against THOMAS COLLINS, otherwise called I THOMAS COLLINS of Loudoun County, Deft.   In Case
Discontinued, the Plt. not further prosecuting

- JANE ASHTON, Admrx. of HENRY ASHTON, deced., Plt. against JOHN KING, Deft.   In Case
This day came Plt. by WILLIAM ELLZEY, her Attorney, and thereupon came also a Jury, to wit

WILLIAM WOLLARD	JAMES ABBETT	WILLIAM STEPHENS
WILLIAM ROSS	JOHN WINN	CHRISTOPHER PERFECT
THOMAS FIELDS	EDWARD HARDEN	THOMAS LEWIS
THOMAS OWSLEY	JOHN LEWIS and	GEORGE CHILTON,

who being elected tried and sworn well and truly to enquire of damages in this suit, went out of Court to consult of their verdict

- NEWDIGATE OWSLEY, an Evidence for THOMAS BOTTS against CHARLES CHINN, having attended Court two daies in March last past and the suit being continued for the Deft., and at his costs, it is ordered that said CHARLES pay him fifty pounds of tobacco for the same

- Indentures of Lease and Release between FRANCIS ELLGINE, Gent., and REBECCA his Wife of the one part and ROBERT ADAM, Gent. of the other part and the Receipt thereon endorsed were acknowledged by the said FRANCIS and acknowledged by the said REBECCA, she having been first privily examined as the Law directs, and together with the said Lease and Receipt ordered to be recorded

- Ordered that a Licence be granted unto WILLIAM DODD to keep an ORDINARY at his House in LEESBURGH for one year, he with Security having entered into Bond as the Law directs

- On motion of WILLIAM COLCLOUGH, who made Oath according to Law, and together with WILLIAM ELLZEY, his Security, entered into and acknowledged Bond, Certificate is granted him for obtaining Letters of Administration on the Estate of ROBERT COLCLOUGH, deceased, in due form

- Ordered that BENJAMIN GRAYSON, Gent., JEREMIAH HUTCHISON, JOHN HUTCHISON and DANIEL HUTCHISON, or any three thereof being first sworn before a Justice of this County, do appraise in current money the slaves (if any) and personal Estate of ROBERT COLCLOUGH, deced., and return the Appraisment to the Court

p. 461   Loudoun County Court 10th of June 1761

- THOMAS HARRISON, JAMES NISBET, BENJAMIN GRAYSON and SPENCE GRAYSON, Executors of the Last Will and Testament of BENJAMIN GRAYSON, Gent., deced., Plts. against GEORGE HANCOCKE, Deft. In Case

The parties by their Attornies mutually submit all matters and Accounts in difference between them to the final determination of PETER WAGENER and HECTOR ROSS, Gent., and agree that their award thereupon to be made the Judgment of the Court and the same is ordered accordingly

- Ordered that the Court be adjourned till tomorrow morning eight o'clock
- The Minutes of these Proceedings were signed

"JAS: HAMILTON"

- At a Court continued and held for Loudoun County at the Courthouse on Thursday the Eleventh day of June one thousand seven hundred and sixty one; Before his Majesty's Justices of the Peace for the said County, to wit,

FIELDING TURNER   JOSIAS CLAPHAM   and
RICHARD COLEMAN   CHARLES TYLER   Gent.

- Indenture of Feofment between NICHOLAS MINOR, Gent., of one part and FRANCIS LIGHTFOOT LEE, Gent., the First Justice named and nominated in the Commission of the Peace for the County of Loudoun for and in behalf of him the said FRANCIS LIGHTFOOT LEE and the rest of the Justices in the said Commission named and their and his Successors of the other part and the Receipt and Memorandum of Livery of Seisen thereon endorsed were acknowledged by the said NICHOLAS and ordered to be recorded

- Present JAMES HAMILTON & AENEAS CAMPBELL, Gent.

- WILLIAM COLVIN, Plt. against JOHN TRAMMELL, Deft.   In Case

By agreement of the parties, this suit is dismissed and it is ordered that Deft. pay unto Plt. his costs

- The Petition of FRANKLIN PERRY against MARGARET JENKINS, Admrx. of SAMUEL JENKINS, deced., is discontinued

p.   Loudoun County Court 11th of June 1761

462   - EZEKIEL HICKMAN, Plt. against JOSHUA HICKMAN, Executor of JOSHUA HICKMAN, deceased, Deft.   In Case

This day came the parties by their Attornies and thereupon all & singular the premises being here seen and fully understood, it appears to the Court that the Errors assigned by Deft. are in Law good and sufficient to arrest Judgment being given on the Verdict aforesaid. Therefore it is considered by the Court that Plt. take nothing by his Bill but for his false clamour be in mercy, &c., and the Deft. go thereof without day and recover against Plt. his costs by him about his defence in this behalf expended; And on the prayer of Plt., an Appeal is granted him to the (blank) day of the next Court, he with WILLIAM ELLZEY, his Security, entered into and acknowledged Bond for the prosecuting the same with effect

- JANE ASHTON, Admrx. of HENRY ASHTON, deced., Plt. agt. JOHN KING, Deft.   In Case

The Jury sworn yesterday to enquire of damages in this suit returned into Court and upon their Oath do say the Plt. hath sustained damages by occasion of Deft.'s Breach of the Promise and Assumption in the Declaration specified to four thousand nine hundred seventy pounds of crop tobacco and one thousand pounds of transfer tobacco besides her costs; Whereupon Deft., by FRANCIS DADE, his Attorney, comes here into Court and prays Judgment on the Verdict aforesaid may be staid and arrested for the following reasons, to wit; "1st. Because the Plt. hath brought the wrong action; 2dly, For that the whole Proceedings are erroneous;" wherefore Deft. prays Judgment on the Verdict aforesaid and that Judgment thereon may be staid and arrested for the reasons aforesaid, And the Plea of Deft. in arrest of Judgment being argued and overruled, it is considered by the Court that Plt. recover against Deft. the damages by the Jury in this Cause assessed and her costs by her about her suit in this behalf expended, and the Deft. in mercy, &c.

- An Indenture of Feofment between NICHOLAS MINOR of one part and WILLIAM DOD of the other part and the Memorandum of Livery of Seisen thereon endorsed were acknowledged by the said NICHOLAS and ordered to be recorded

- An Indenture of Feofment between NICHOLAS MINOR of one part and JOHN HERYFORD of other part and the Memorandum of Livery of Seisen and Receipt thereon endorsed were acknowledged by the said NICHOLAS and ordered to be recorded

- BENJAMIN MASON, an Evidence for JANE ASHTON, Admrx. of HENRY ASHTON, deced., against JOHN KING having attended Court three daies, ordered that said JANE

p.   Loudoun County Court 11th of June 1761
463   pay him seventy five pounds of tobacco for the same

- JAMES INGOE DOZER, Plt. against JAMES GOULDING, Deft.   In Case
Continued till next Court at motion and costs of Plt.

- THOMAS HARRISON, JAMES NISBET, BENJAMIN GRAYSON and
SPENCE GRAYSON, Executors of the Last Will and Testament of BENJA-
MIN GRAYSON, Gent., deced., Plts. against JOHN KING, Deft.   In Case

The Sherif not having executed the former Attachment, on motion of Plt. by his
Attorney, it is ordered that another Attachment issue against the Deft.'s Estate for
four thousand pounds of crop tobacco and fifty shillings current money and costs returnable here at next Court

- FRANCIS PEYTON and NICHOLAS MINOR, Gent., Churchwardens for the
time being for the Parish of Cameron in the County of Loudoun, Plts. agt.
ANN GRIFFIN, Deft.   In Debt

The Deft. being returned not found, on motion of Plt.'s Attorney a Plurius Capias is
awarded them returnable here at the next Court

- GEORGE WEST, Gent., Plt. against WILLIAM STEPHENS, Deft. In Case

This day came the parties by their Attornies and thereupon came also a Jury to
wit;   WILLIAM WOLLARD   JAMES ABBETT   WILLIAM ROSS
      JOHN WINN   THOMAS LEWIS   THOMAS FIELDS
      EDWARD HARDEN   JOHN LEWIS   BENJAMIN MASON
      BENJAMIN EDWARDS   EZEKIEL HICKMAN and   THOMAS PRITCHARD
who being elected tried and sworn the truth to speak upon the issue joined, upon their
Oath do day that Deft. is Not Guilty as in pleading he hath alledged. Therefore it is
considered by the Court that Plt. take nothing by his Bill but for his false clamour be
in mercy, &c., and Deft. go thereof without day and recover against Plt. his costs by
him about his defence in this behalf expended

- JAMES KANNADAY came into Court and acknowledged himself indebted
unto our Sovereign Lord George the Third King of Great Britain, &c., in the sum of ten
pounds of his lands and tenements goods and chattels to be levied and to our said Lord
the King his heirs and successors rendered, Yet upon condition that if JAMES
KANNADAY shall be of good behavior towards the King and all his Liege People for
the space of one year from this time this Recognizance to be void

p.   Loudoun County Court 11th of June 1761
464   - RICHARD SNOWDEN, Plt. against BENJAMIN MUSGROVE, Deft.
          In Case

The Deft. being returned not found, on motion of Plt.'s Attorney a Plurius Capias is
awarded him returnable here at next Court

- RICHARD SNOWDEN, Plt. against BENJAMIN MUSGROVE, otherwise
called I BENJAMIN MUSGROVE of ANN ARUNDELL County, Deft.
In Debt

The Deft. being returned not found, on motion of Plt.'s Attorney a Plurius Capias is
awarded him returnable here at next Court

- JOHN HOUGH, Executor of the Last Will & Testament of JOHN POULT-
NEY, deced., Plt. against WILLIAM COLVILL, Deft.   In Case

JOSIAS CLAPHAM, Gent. comes into Court and undertakes for Deft. that in case
he shall be cast in this suit he shall pay and satisfy the condemnation of the Court or

render his body to Prison in execution for the same, or that he, the said JOSIAS, will do it for him; And Deft. by WILLIAM ELLZEY, his Attorney, saving to himself all advantages of Exceptions as well to Plt.'s Writ as to his Declaration prays and has leave to imparl till next Court and then to plead

> - CHRISTOPHER PERFECT, Plt. against JACOB PFHAW, otherwise called I JACOB PFHAW of the County of Loudoun and Colony of Virginia, Deft. In Debt

By agreement of the parties, this suit is dismissed and it is ordered that Deft. pay unto Plt. his costs

> - REBECCA EADES, an Infant under the age of twenty one years, by THOMAS HAMILTON, her Guardian and next Friend, Plt. against JOHN LACKEY and JACOB GARDNER, Defts.   In Trespass Assault and Battery

The Deft., JACOB GARDNER being returned not found, on motion of Plt.'s Attorney, a Plurius Capias is awarded him returnable here at next Court

> - THOMAS OWSLEY, an Evidence for WILLIAM STEPHENS at the suit of GEORGE WEST, Gent., having attended Court four daies, ordered that said WILLIAM pay him one hundred pounds of tobacco for the same

> - Ordered that WILLIAM HUTCHISON be appointed CONSTABLE in the room of JAMES LEITH who is discharged from that Office

p.   Loudoun County Court 11th of June 1761
465   - ROBERT WOOD, an Evidence for WILLIAM STEPHENS at the suit of GEORGE WEST, Gent., having attended Court four daies, ordered that said WILLIAM pay him one hundred pounds of tobacco for the same

> - NICHOLAS MINOR and FRANCIS PEYTON, Gent., Churchwardens for the time being for the Parish of Cameron in the County of Loudoun who sue for the use of the Parish, Plts. against MARY WINSOR, Deft.   In Debt

The Deft. being arrested and not appearing, on motion of Plts. by their Attorney, it is ordered that unless Deft. shall appear here at next Court and answer the action of Plts., Judgment shall be then given for Plts. against her for the Debt in the Declaration mentioned and costs

> - FRANCIS PEYTON and NICHOLAS MINOR, Gent., Churchwardens for the time being for the Parish of Cameron in the County of Loudoun, Plts. against ANN CORNWELL, Deft.   In Debt

Discontinued, the Plts. not further prosecuting

> - CRAVEN PEYTON, Assignee of ARTHUR CHARLTON, Plt. agt. JOSEPH CLAYPOOLE, otherwise called I JOSEPH CLAYPOOLE of FAIRFAX County in the Colony of Virginia, Farmer, Deft.   In Debt

Continued till the next Court

> - Ordered that WILLIAM TRIPLETT, DANIEL ADAMS, WILLIAM SMITH and THOMAS LEWIS, or andy three thereof being first sworn before a Justice of this County do view the most convenient way for a Road from the FORD over LITTLE RIVER to ASHBY' GAP and make a report of the conveniency and inconveniency that will attend the same to the Court

> - Ordered that WILLIAM TAYLOR, WILLIAM SMITH, THOMAS LEWIS and ROBERT WOOD or any three thereof being first sworn before a Justice of this County do view the most convenient way for a Road from LASSWELL's FORD to

the MOUNTAIN ROAD by ROBERT WOOD's and make a report of the conveniency and inconveniency that will attend the same to the Court
- Ordered that the Court be adjourned till tomorrow morning eight o'clock
- The Minutes of these Proceedings were signed
"JAS: HAMILTON"

p.   - At a Court continued and held for Loudoun County on Friday the Twelfth
466 day of June one thousand seven hundred and sixty one, Before his Majesty's
     Justices of the Peace for the said County, to wit;
     AENEAS CAMPBELL   RICHARD COLEMAN &
     WILLIAM WEST   GEORGE WEST   Gentlemen

- ABRAHAM BARNES, Plt. against FRANKLIN PERRY, Deft.   In Case
The Plt. not further prosecuting, on motion of Deft. by his Attorney, it is ordered that this suit be discontinued and that Plt. pay unto Deft. his costs
- ANDREW ADAM, Plt. agt. MICHAEL VAN BUSKIRK, Deft.   In Case
JOHN ST. CLAIR and WILLIAM WOLLARD both of this County come into Court and undertake for Deft. that in case he shall be cast in this suit he shall pay and satisfy the condemnation of the Court or render his body to Prison in execution for the same or that they, the said JOHN and WILLIAM, will do it for him; And Deft., by WILLIAM ELLZEY, his Attorney, saving to himself all advantages of Exceptions as well to Plt.'s Writ as to his Declaration, prays and has leave to imparl till next Court and then to plead
- WILLIAM BLACK, Plt. agt. JACOB BEASON, Deft.   In Case
This day came the parties by their Attornies and Deft. saving to himself all advantages of Exceptions as well to Plt.'s Writ as to his Declaration prays and has leave to imparl till next Court and then to plead
- BENJAMIN GRAYSON and CRAVEN PEYTON, Plts. against
JOHN BISHOP, Deft.   In Case
By agreement of the parties, this suit is dismissed and it is ordered that Deft. pay unto Plts. their costs
- WILLIAM MURPHEY, Plt. against THOMAS STUMP, Executor of the
Last Will and Testament of ROBERT BOOTH, deced., Deft.   In Case
This day came the parties by their Attornies and Deft. saving to himself all

p.   Loudoun County Court 12th of June 1761
467 advantages of Exceptions as well to Plt.'s Writ as to his Declaration prays
     and has leave to imparl till next Court and then to plead
     - ISAAC HOLLINGSWORTH, JOHN HOUGH and ELIONER POULTNEY,
     Exrs. of the Last Will and Testament of JOHN POULTNEY, deced., Plts.
     against DAVID DAVIS and EZEKIEL HICKMAN, Defts.   In Debt
NICHOLAS MINOR, Gent., comes into Court and undertakes for Defts. that in case they shall be cast in this suit that they will pay and satisfy the condemnation of the Court or render his body to Prison in execution for the same or that he, the said NICHOLAS, will do it for him; And Deft. by WILLIAM ELLZEY, his Attorney, saving to himself all advantages of Exceptions as well to Plt.'s Writ as to his Declaration, prays and has leave to imparl till next Court and then to plead

- DAVID ROSS, Plt. against JOHN ROSS DEWITT, otherwise called I
JOHN ROSS DEWITT of FAIRFAX County, Deft.   In Debt
Continued till next Court

- JOSIAS CLAPHAM, Gent., Plt. against SAMUEL PATTERSON, Deft.
In Case
This day came the parties by their Attornies and Deft. saving to himself all advantages of Exceptions as well to Plt.'s Writ as to his Declaration, prays and has leave to imparl till next Court and then to plead

- ANDREW ADAM, Plt. agt. THOMAS PHILLIPS, Deft.   In Debt
The Deft. being returned not found, on motion of Plt.'s Attorney an Alias Capias is awarded him returnable here at next Court

- NICHOLAS MINOR and JAMES LANE, Gent., Churchwardens for the
Parish of Cameron in the County of Loudoun for the time being, who sue for
the use of the Parish, Plts. agt. ANN HAYS, Deft.   In Debt
The Deft. being arrested and not appearing, on motion of Plts. by their Attorney, it is ordered that unless Deft. shall appear at next Court and answer the action of Plts., Judgment shall be then given for Plts. against her for the Debt in the Declaration mentioned and costs

p.   Loudoun County Court 12th of June 1761
468   - JOSIAS CLAPHAM, Gent., Plt. against THOMAS JONES, Deft.
In Trespass
The Deft. being returned not found, on motion of Plt.'s Attorney, an Alias Capias is awarded him returnable here at next Court

- JOHN SASSER, Plt. against NATHAN WILLIAMSON, Deft.
In Trespass Assault and Battery
This day came the parties by their Attornies and Deft. saving to himself all advantages of Exceptions as well to Plt.'s Writ as to his Declaration, prays and has leave to imparl till next Court and then to plead

- JOHN SASSER, Plt. against NATHAN WILLIAMSON, Deft.   In Case
This day came the parties by their Attornies and Deft. saving to himself all advantages of Exceptions as well to Plt.'s Writ as to his Declaration, prays and has leave to imparl till next Court and then to plead

- ROBERT and ANDREW ADAM, Plts. against SAMUEL HARRIS, Deft.
In Case
By agreement of the parties, this suit is dismissed and it is ordered that Deft. pay unto Plts. their costs

- JOHN HARDEN, Gent., Plt. against JOHN DAVIS, otherwise called I
JOHN DAVIS of Loudoun County, Farmer, Deft.   In Debt
THOMAS PRITCHARD comes into Court and undertakes for Deft. that in case he shall be cast in this suit that he will pay and satisfy the condemnation of the Court or render his body to Prison in execution for the same, or that he, the said THOMAS, will do it for him; And Deft. by FRANCIS DADE, his Attorney, saving to himself all advantages of Exception as well to Plt.'s Writ as to his Declaration prays and has leave to imparl till next Court and then to plead

- GEORGE FLING, Plt. agt. JOHN HARLE, Deft.   In Case
This day came the parties by their Attornies and Deft. saving to himself all advan-

tages of Exception as well to Plt.'s Writ as to his Declaration prays and has leave to imparl till next Court and then to plead

p.   Loudoun County Court 12th of June 1761
469   - JOSEPH YATES, Plt. agt. SAMUEL BISHOP, Deft.   In Case
This day came the parties by their Attornies and Deft. saving to himself all advantages of Exceptions as well to Plt.'s Writ as to his Declaration, prays and has leave to imparl till next Court and then to plead
    - WILLIAM DODD, Plt. agt. JAMES ABBETT, Deft.   In Case
This day came the parties by their Attornies and Deft. saving to himself all advantages of Exception as well to Plt.'s Writ as to his Declaration, prays and has leave to imparl till next Court and then to plead
    - HENRY BREWER, Plt. agt. ARTHUR MORTIMORE, Deft.   In Case
This day came the parties by their Attornies and Deft. saving to himself all advantages of Exceptions as well to Plt.'s Writ as to his Declaration, prays and has leave to imparl till next Court and then to plead
    - JOHN HERYFORD, Plt. agt. JOHN SPURGEN, Deft.
    In Trespass Assault and Battery
This day came the parties by their Attornies and Deft. saving to himself all advantages of Exceptions as well to Plt.'s Writ as to is Declaration, prays and has leave to imparl till next Court and then to plead
    - ROBERT ADAM, Assignee of JOHN HUNTER, Plt. agt.
    WILLIAM OWSLEY, Deft.   In Debt
The Deft. being arrested and not appearing, on motion of Plt. by HUGH WEST, his Attorney, it is ordered that unless Deft. shall appear here at next Court and answer Plt.'s action, Judgment shall be then given for Plt. against im for the Debt in the Declaration mentoned and costs
    - RODHAM NEALE, Plt. agt. PHILIP NOLAND, Deft.   In Debt
This day came the parties by their Attornies, and Deft. saving to himself all advantages of Exceptions as well to Plt.'s Writ as to his Declaration, prays and has leave to imparl till next Court and then to plead

p.   Loudoun County Court 12th of June 1761
470   - JOHN CHRISTOPHER CANNOUSE, Plt. against DANIEL DAVIS,
    Deft.   In Case
This suit is dismissed, being agreed by the parties
    - JAMES ABIT and ANN his Wife, and JANE McDOWELL, Executors of the
    Last Will and Testament of MARY JENNINGS, deced., Plts. against
    WILLIAM DODD, Deft.   In Debt
This day came the parties by their Attornies, and Deft. saving to himself all advantages of Exceptions as well to Plts.'s Writ as to their Declaration, prays and has leave to imparl till next Court and then to plead
    - Aminidab Goodtitle, Lessee of JOHN WATSON, Plt. against
    Ferdinando Badtitle, Deft.   In Ejectment for one messuage and one hundred fifty acres of land with the appurtenances lying and being in the Parish of Cameron and County of Loudoun;
LEWIS ELLZEY on his motion is admitted Deft. in this suit in the room of said

Badtitle and thereupon by WILLIAM ELLZEY, his Attorney, he comes and defends the force and injury when, &c., pleads the general issue and confesses Lease Entry & Ouster in the Declaration supposed and agrees to insist on the Title at the Trial only, and for Trial thereof puts himself upon the Country and Plt. likewise, Therefore it is commanded the Sherif that he cause to come here at next Court twelve good and lawful men by whom, &c.

FRANCIS DADE here in Court undertakes for Plt. that in case Plt. shall be cast in this suit, he shall pay and satisfy all such damages costs and charges as shall be awarded against him or that he will pay them for him

     - WILLIAM MURPHY, Plt. against THOMAS KELLEY, Deft. In Case

The Deft. pleads Not Guilty which the Plt. joins and Deft. for further Plea says that he is Not Guilty of the premises laid to his charge within one year before the bringing of this suit, which Plt. joines and the Trial is referred till next Court

     - THOMAS KELLEY, Plt. agt. THOMAS FIELDS, Deft.   In Case

The Plt. not further prosecuting, on motion of Deft. by HUGH WEST, his Attorney, it is ordered that the suit be discontinued and that Plt. pay unto Deft. his costs

p.   <u>Loudoun County Court 12th of June 1761</u>
471   - DENNIS DALLIS, Plt. against JOHN PYLES, Deft.

     In Trespass Assault and Battery

This day came the parties by their Attornies and Deft. saving to himself all advantages of Exceptions as well to Plt.'s Writ as to his Declaration, prays and has leave to imparl till next Court and then to plead

     - SARAH LEWIS, Widow and Relict of THOMAS LEWIS, deced., Complt.
     against ELIZABETH LEWIS, Deft.   In Chancery

WILLIAM DOUGLAS, who since the bringing of this suit intermarried with the Deft., is admitted Deft. with her and on their motion time is allowed them till next Court to answer the Complainant's Bill

     - JOHN DAVIS and MARGARET his Wife, late MARGARET DAVIS, Admrx.
     &c., of THOMAS DAVIS the Eldest, deced., Plts. agt. ELIZABETH DAVIS,
     Admrx. &c. of THOMAS DAVIS the Younger, Deft. In Case

The Deft. saith she is Not Guilty and for Trial thereof putteth herself upon the Country and Plts. likewise, Therefore it is commanded that the Sherif cause to come here at the next Court twelve good and lawful men by whom, &c.

     - ELIZABETH LEWIS, Complt. agt. JOHN DAVIS and MARGARET his
     Wife, late MARGARET DAVIS, Widow and Relict of THOMAS DAVIS,
     SENR., late of Loudoun County and Colony of Virginia, Planter, Defts.
     In Chancery

This suit abates by the Marriage of the Complainant

     - BENJAMIN GRAYSON and STACEY his Wife, Admrx. of BURGESS
     BERKLEY, deced., Complts. agt. WILLIAM BERKLEY, Deft. In Chancery

The Deft. failing to answer Complts.'s Bill, it is ordered that an Attachment be issued against him returnable here at the next Court

     - BENJAMIN SEBASTIAN, Complt. against CHARLES ESKRIDGE, Deft.
     In Chancery

Continued till next Court at motion and costs of Complt.

- BENJAMIN GRAYSON, Gent., Plt. against JOHN DAVIS, Deft. In Case
On motion and costs of Plt., further time is allowed him till next Court to file his
Declaration

p.   Loudoun County Court 12th of June 1761
472   - HENRY PEYTON, Gent., Plt. against SAMUEL STILLWELL, Deft.
         In Case
The Deft. saith that he is Not Guilty and for Trial thereof putteth himself upon the
Country and Plt. likewise. Therefore it is commanded that the Sherif cause to come
at the next Court twelve good and lawful men by whom, &c.
         - JOSEPH MAYSE, Plt. agt. BENJAMIN GRAYSON, otherwise called I
         BENJAMIN GRAYSON of SPOTSYLVANIA County, Deft.   In Debt
The Deft. pleads paiment and for Trial thereof putteth himself upon the County and
Plt. likewise. Therefore it is commaned that the Sherif cause to come at the next
Court twelve good and lawful men by whom, &c.
         - HENRY WISHEART, Plt. agt. JOHN DAVIS, otherwise called I JOHN
         DAVIS of Loudoun County, Deft.   In Debt
This day came the parties by their Attornies and Deft. acknowledged Plt.'s action
for three pounds, fourteen shillings. Therefore with the assent of Plt., it is considered
by the Court that Plt. recover against Deft. three pounds fourteen shillings with lawful Interest thereon from the 1st day of October 1758 till paid, and also his costs by
him in this behalf expended and the Deft. in mercy, &c.
         - JOHN GLADIN, Plt. agt. JOSEPH CLAYPOLE, Deft. In Case
The parties by their Attornies mutually submit all matters in difference between
them in this suit to the final determination of WILLIAM ELLZEY and HUGH WEST
and agree that their Award thereupon to be made the Judgment of the Court and the
same is ordered accordingly
         - ARCHIBALD CAMPBELL, Clerk, Plt. agt. JOHN ANDREWS, otherwise
         called I JOHN ANDREWS of the Parish of Cameron and County of FAIRFAX,
         Clerk, Deft.   In Debt
The Deft. pleads paiment and for Trial thereof putteth himself upon the Country
and Plt. likewise; Therefore it is commanded that the Sherif cause to come at the
next Court twelve good and lawful men by whom, &c.

p.   Loudoun County Court 12th of June 1761
473   ALEXANDER YOUNG & COMPANY, Plts. against JOSIAS CLAPHAM,
         Deft.   In Case
The Deft. saith he did not assume upon himself in manner and form as Plts. against
him hath complained, and for this he putteth himself upon the Country, and Plts. likewise; and the Trial is referred till the next Court
         - JAMES LEITH, Plt. agt. JAMES INGO DOZER, Deft.   In Case
The Deft. saith he is Not Guilty and for Trial thereof putteth himself upon the
Country and Plt. likewise; Therefore it is commanded that the Sherif cause to come
at the next Court twelve good and lawful men by whom &c.
         - ALEXANDER FARROW, Plt. against RICHARD FREEMAN and
         ELIZABETH FREEMAN, Defts.   In Case
The Deft., ELIZABETH, saith that she is Not Guilty and for Trial thereof the Defts.

put themselves upon the Country and Plt. likewise, Therefore it is commanded that the Sherif cause to come to the next Court twelve good and lawful men by whom, &c.

    - ROBERT EASTHAM, Plt. agt. THOMAS BOTTS, Deft.   In Debt

The Deft. pleads paiment and for Trial putteth himself upon the Country and Plt. likewise, Therefore it is commanded that the Sherif cause to come here at the next Court twelve good and lawful men by whom, &c.

    - JOSIAS CLAPHAM, Gent., Plt. against EZEKIEL HICKMAN, Deft. In Case

The Deft. saith he is Not Guilty and for Trial putteth himself upon the Country and Plt. likewise; Therefore it is commanded that the Sherif cause to come here at the next Court twelve good and lawful men by whom, &c.

    - JAMES MACCUBBIN, Plt. against JOHN SHEPHERD, Deft. In Debt

The Deft. pleads paiment and for Trial thereof putteth himself upon the Country and Plt. likewise, Therefore it is commanded that the Sherif cause to come here at next Court twelve good and lawful men by whom, &c.

p.   Loudoun County Orders 1757-1762

474   - ROBERT CARTER, Esqr., Plt. against EDWARD MASTERSON, Deft. In Case

The Deft. pleads paiment and for Trial thereof putteth himself upon the Country and Plt. likewise; Therefore it is commanded that the Sherif cause to come here at the next Court twelve good and lawful men by whom, &c.

    - JAMES ROGERS, Plt. agt. SAMUEL WINN, Deft. In Trespass

The Deft. saith he is Not Guilty and for Trial thereof putteth himself upon the Country and Plt. likewise; Therefore it is commanded that the Sherif cause to come here at the next Court twelve good and lawful men by whom, &c.

    - JAMES ROGERS, Plt. agt. JOHN HALL, Deft.   In Trespass

The Deft. saith he is Not Guilty and for Trial thereof putteth himself upon the Country and Plt. likewise; Therefore it is commanded that the Sherif cause to come here at the next Court twelve good and lawful men by whom, &c.

    - THOMAS MOXLEY, Plt. agt. JOHN TRAMMELL, Deft.   In Case

The Deft. saith he is Not Guilty and for Trial thereof putteth himself upon the Country and Plt. likewise, Therefore it is commanded that the Sherif cause to come here at the next Court twelve good and lawful men by whom, &c.

    - LEVEN POWELL, Plt. against JOHN OWSLEY, Deft.
In Trespass Assault and Battery

The Deft. saith he is Not Guilty and for Trial thereof putteth himself upon the Country and Plt. likewise; Therefore it is commanded that the Sherif cause to come here at the next Court twelve good and lawful men by whom, &c.

    - SIMON PEARSON and MILKEY PEARSON his Wife; WILLIAM STARKE and SUSANNA STARKE his Wife, EZEKIEL HICKMAN and ELIZABETH HICKMAN his Wife and WILLIAM TRAMMELL, Complts against JOHN TRAMMELL and SAMPSON TRAMMELL, Defts.
In Chancery

On motion of Defts. further time is allowed them till the next Court to answer the Bill of the Complainants

p.   Loudoun County Court 12th of June 1761
475   - Messrs. ROBERT DREGHORN & COMPANY of Great Britain, Plts. agt.
       JOHN NEAVILL JUNR. otherwise called I JOHN NEAVILL, JUNR. of
       PRINCE WILLIAM County, Deft.   In Debt
This day came Plts. by WILLIAM ELLZEY their Attorney and Deft. not appearing
and failing to give Special Bail, on motion of Plts. by their Attorney, it is considered by
the Court that Plts. recover against Deft. and JAMES SPENCER & JOHN MED-
CAP, the Securities for his appearance, six pounds, four shillings and two pence, the
Debt in the Declaration mentioned and their costs by them in this behalf expended;
And Deft. in mercy, &c., But this Judgment is to be discharged by the paiment of
three pounds, two shillings and one penny together with Interest for the same to be
computed after the rate of five percentum per annum from the first day of December
1755 till time of paiment and the costs
       - HUGH WEST, Plt. agt. RODHAM NEALE, Deft.   In Case
The Deft. filed a Demurrer which Plt. joins and the Cause is continued till next
Court
       - THOMAS MIDDLETON, Plt. agt. JOHN WINN, Deft.   In Debt
The Deft. filed a Demurrer which Plt. joins and the Cause is continued till next
Court
       - GERARD ALEXANDER, Gent., Plt. agt. GEORGE WEST, Deft. In Case
The Deft. saith he did not assume upon himself in manner and form as Plt. against
him hath complained and of this he putteth himself upon the Country and Plt. like-
wise, and the Trial is referred till the next Court
       - The Petition of FRANCIS JOHNSON against JOHN KING is continued till
the next Court
       - WILLIAM CARR, Gent., Plt. against JAMES GOULDING, Deft.   In Case
The Sherif not having executed the former Attachment, on motion of Plt.'s Attorney, it is ordered that another Attachment issue against Deft.'s Estate for nine
pounds, sixteen shillings and two pence and costs returnable here at next Court
       - An Account of the Administration of the Estate of JOHN RATCLIFF, deced.,
was returned into Court by SUSANNA RATCLIFF, the Admrx., to which she made
Oath and the same being examined and approved of by the Court, is ordered to be
recorded

p.   Loudoun County Court 12th of June 1762
476   - Present. FRANCIS PEYTON, Gent.
       - ABRAHAM BARNES, Plt. against SAMPSON TURLEY, Deft. In Case
This day came the parties by their Attornies and thereupon the matters of Law
arising upon the Special Verdict in this Cause being argued; It seems to the Court
here that the Law is for the Deft. Therefore it is considered by the Court that Plt.
take nothing by his Bill but for his false clamour be in mercy, &c., And the Deft. go
hence without day and recover against Plt. his costs by him about his defence in this
behalf expended
       - JOHN CRAIG, Admr. of all and singular the goods and chattels rights &
       credits which were of DAVID CRAIG, deced., Plt. against THOMAS
       AWBREY, Deft.   Upon a Writ of Scire Facias
This day came the parties by their Attornies and Deft. relinquishing his former Plea

saith that he cannot gainsay Plt.'s action. Therefore it is considered by the Court that Plt. have execution against Deft. for two thousand six hundred fifty one pounds of crop tobacco, two pounds ten shillings and ten pence half penny current money and three hundred eighteen pounds of tobacco and fifteen shillings or one hundred fifty pounds of tobacco and also his costs by him in this behalf expended, and Deft. in mercy &c.

      - JAMES NISBET, Plt. agt. JAMES LEITH, Deft.   In Case

   This day came the parties by their Attornies and thereupon came also a Jury to wit;

WILLIAM WOLLARD	BENJAMIN EDWARDS	JAMES ABBET
JOHN SHEPHERD	JOHN TRAMMELL	WILLIAM ROSS
HUGH FOUCH	JOHN DAVIS	JOHN ST. CLAIR
JOHN THOMAS	DAVID DAVIS and	THOMAS PRITCHARD

who being elected tried and sworn the truth to speak upon the issue joined, went out of Court to consult of their Verdict

      - Indentures of Lease and Release between EDWARD HARDEN and MARY his Wife of the one part and GEORGE GREGG of the other part were acknowledged by the said EDWARD and MARY, she having been first privily examined as the Law directs, and the Receipt thereon endorsed was acknowledged by the said EDWARD and together eith the Indentures ordered to be recorded

      - JAMES INGOE DOZER, Plt. against JAMES LEITH, Deft.   In Case

   This day came the parties by their Attornies and Deft. relinquishes his

p.   Loudoun County Court 12th of June 1761

477   former Plea and saith that he did not assume upon himself in manner and form as Plt. against him hath declared and of this he putteth himself upon the Counrty, and Plt. likewise, and the Trial is referred till next Court

      - Ordered that the Court be adjourned till the second Tuesday in July next

      - The Minutes of these Proceedings were signed

                           "AENS: CAMPBELL"

      - At a Court held for Loudoun County at the Courthouse on Tuesday the Fourteenth day of July in the first year of the Reign of our Sovereign Lord George the Third by the grace of God of Great Britain France and Ireland, King, Defender of the faith, &c., Annoque Domini one thousand seven hundred and sixty one Before his Majesty's Justices of the Peace for the said County, to wit.

FIELDING TURNER	RICHARD COLEMAN &
AENEAS CAMPBELL	JAMES LANE, Gent.

      - An Indenture of Feofment between WILLIAM BERRY of the one part and JAMES MURRAY of the other part and the Memorandum of Livery of Seisin and Receipt thereon endorsed were acknowledged by the said WILLIAM (and REBECCA the Wife of said WILLIAM being first privately examined, relinquished her Right of Dower to the lands and premises conveyed by the Indenture) which are ordered to be recorded

      - An Indenture of Feofment between WILLIAM GLADIN and MARY his Wife of the one part and JOHN TRAMMELL of the other part and the Memorandum of Livery of Seisin and Receipt thereunder written were proved by the Oath of BENJAMIN SEBASTIAN, JUNR. a witness thereto, and the same having been before proved by the Oaths of BENJAMIN SEBASTIAN and FRANCIS DADE, witnesses thereto, and together with a Commission for taking the acknowledgment and privy examination of the said MARY, and the Certificate of the execution thereof, ordered to be recorded

- An Indenture of Lease between JOHN CARLYLE and JOHN DALTON, Gent., of the one part and JOHN CARR of the other part was acknowledged by JOHN CARLYLE to be his act and deed and likewise to be the act and deed of JOHN DALTON and is ordered to be recorded

- An Indenture of Lease between JOHN CARLYLE, Attorney in Fct for GEORGE WILLIAM FAIRFAX, Esqr., of the one part and WILLIAM WILDMAN of the other part was acknowledged by JOHN CARLYLE and is ordered to be recorded

p.   Loudoun County Court 14th of July 1761
478   - An Indenture of Lease between JOHN CARLYLE, Attorney in Fact for
        GEORGE WILLIAM FAIRFAX, Esqr., of the one part and JACOB SHO-
MAKER of the other part was acknowledged by JOHN CARLYLE and is ordered to be recorded

- An Indenture of Lease between JOHN CARLYLE, Attorney in Fact for GEORGE WILLIAM FAIRFAX, Esqr., of the one part and JOSEPH BURSON of the other part was acknowledged by JOHN CARLYLE and is ordered to be recorded

- ROBERT CARTER, Esqr. Plt. agt. EDWARD MASTERSON, Deft. In Case This suit is dismissed, being agreed by the parties

- An Indenture of Lease between JOHN CARLYLE, Attorney in Fact for GEORGE WILLIAM FAIRFAX, Esqr., of the one part and JAMES CUNARD of the other part was acknowledged by JOHN CARLYLE and is ordered to be recorded

- An Indenture of Lease between JOHN CARLYLE, Attorney in Fact for GEORGE WILLIAM FAIRFAX, Esqr. of the one part and SAMUEL PHILLIPS of the other part was acknowledged by JOHN CARLYLE and is ordered to be recorded

- An Indenture of Lease between JOHN CARLYLE, Attorney in Fact for GEORGE WILLIAM FAIRFAX, Esqr., of the one part and MATTHIAS GOSSETT of the other part was acknowledged by JOHN CARLYLE and is ordered to be recorded

- Upon the Proceedings taken and returned against JACOB SHILLING on Suspicion of being Guilty of taking a Bell on the King's Highway, the property of ROBERT WORTHINGTON, the said JACOB appeared according to his Recognizance. Whereupon said ROBERT was sworn and examined against said JACOB and he heard in his defence. On consideration whereof it is the opinion of the Court that said JACOB is Not Guilty of the Fact laid to his charge and thereupon is acquitted and discharged from his Recognizance aforesaid

- Upon the Petition of JOHN HOUGH for leave to build a Water Griss Mill over GOOSE CREEK in this County near where the Main Road crosses said Creek at the Lower Ford and also to have one acre of land laid off adjacent thereto belonging to (blank) SELDEN, it is ordered that the Sherif summon a Jury of twelve Freeholders of the Vicinage to meet upon the land petitioned for who being met and duly sworn before a Magistrate or the Sherif shall diligently view and examined the said land and the lands adjacent thereto on both sides the Run which may be affected or laid under water by building such Mill, together with the Timber and other conveniences thereon and report the same with the true value of the acre petitioned for and of the damages to the party holding the same or to any other person or persons under their hands and seals to the Court

p.   Loudoun County Court 14th of July 1761
479   - CORNELIUS VAUNE exhibited an Account against JANE McDANIEL,
       a Runaway Servant, for four daies absent time and one hundred sixty pounds of tobacco and fifteen shillings nine pence in taking of her up which being proved and allowed in Court, it is ordered that said JANE do serve her said Master for the same according to Law after her time by Indenture Custom or former Order of Court shall be fully expired and that she pay the costs, &c.
       - CORNELIUS VAUNE exhibited an Account against MARGARET WATSON, a Runaway Servant, for four daies absent time and one hundred sixty pounds of tobacco and fifteen shillings nine pence expended in taking of her up which being approved and allowed by the Court, it is ordered that said MARGARET do serve her said Master for the same according to Law after her time by Indenture custom or former Order of Court shall be fully expired and that said MARGARET pay the costs, &c.
       - Indentures of Lease and Release between JOHN HANCOCK, Gent., of one part and THOMAS BROWN and the Receipt thereon endorsed were acknowledged by said JOHN and ordered to be recorded
       - An Indenture of Release of Dower between ELIZABETH AWBREY, Widow and Relict of HENRY AWBREY, deced., of the one part and ANN PHILLIPS, Widow and Relict of JOHN PHILLIPS, deced., of the other part, was acknowledged by said ELIZABETH and is ordered to be recorded
       - An Indenture of Release of Dower between ELIZABETH AWBREY, Widow and Relict of HENRY AWBREY, deced., of the one part and JOSIAS CLAPHAM, GENT., of the other part was acknowledged by said ELIZABETH and is ordered to be recorded
       - Indentures of Lease and Release between PHILIP PHILIPS of the one part and JOSIAS CLAPHAM of the other part and the Receipt thereon endorsed were proved by the Oath of JOSEPH FARRELL, a witness thereto
       - An Indenture of Lease between JOHN CARLYLE, Gent., Attorney in Fact for GEORGE WILLIAM FAIRFAX, Esqr., of the one part and JOHN COMPTON of the other part was acknowledged by JOHN CARLYLE and is ordered to be recorded
       - An Account of Administration of the Estate of SAMUEL JENKINS, deceased, was returned into Court by MARGARET JENKINS, the Administratrix, to which she made Oath and the same examined and approved of by the Court is ordered to be recorded
       - An Indenture of Lease between JOHN CARLYLE, Gent., Attorney in Fact for GEORGE WILLIAM FAIRFAX, Esqr., of the one part and JOHN NOWLAND of the other part was acknowledged by JOHN CARLYLE and ordered to be recorded
           - Present FRANCIS PEYTON, Gent.
       - An Indenture of Lease between JOHN CARLYLE, Gent., Attorney in Fact for GEORGE WILLIAM FAIRFAX, Esqr., of the one part and FRANCIS BALDWIN of the other part was acknowledged by JOHN CARLYLE and ordered to be recorded
       - An Inventory and Appraisment of the Estate of HENRY INSLEY, deceased, was returned into Court and is ordered to be recorded

p.   Loudoun County Court 14th of July 1761
480   - BENJAMIN SEBASTIAN, JUNR., a witness to prove a Deed of Feofment
        between WILLIAM GLADIN and MARY his Wife of the one part and JOHN
TRAMMELL of the other part having attended Court one day and for travelling forty
miles from FAIRFAX County and returning, ordered that said JOHN pay him one
hundred forty five pounds of tobacco for the same
        - The Petition of JOHN TRAMMELL against WILLIAM COLVIN is discon-
tinued
        - WILLIAM CARR, Gent., Plt. agt. JAMES GOULDING, Deft.   In Case
   This day came as well Plt. by WILLIAM ELLZEY his Attorney as Deft. in his proper person and Deft. acknowledged Plt.'s action for nine pounds, sixteen shillings and
two pence. Therefore with the assent of Plt., it is considered by the Court that Plt.
recover against Deft. the nine pounds, sixteen shillings and two pence and his costs by
him in this behalf expended, and the Deft. in mercy, &c.
        - JAMES NISBET, Plt. agt. JAMES LEITH, Deft.   In Case
   The Jury impannelled and sworn in this Cause at the last Court failing to appear
being called, the suit is continued till next Court
        - A Bill of Sale from FERDINANDO NEAL to JAMES LANE, JUNR., was
acknowledged by said FERDINANDO and is ordered to be recorded
        - Bess, a Negro girl belonging to THOMAS OWSLEY, adjudged by the Court to
be ten years of age
        - Upon Petition of FIELDING TURNER, Gent., against CLATER SMITH for
a Debt due by Account, this day came the parties by their Attornies, who being fully
heard, it is considered by the Court that Plt. recover against Deft. one pound, six shillings and eleven pence three farthings and his costs in this behalf expended
        - Ordered that a Licence be granted JOHN HERYFORD to keep an ORDI-
NARY at his House for one year from this time, he with Security having entered into
Bond as the Law directs
        - THOMAS COCKRILL an Evidence for FIELDING TURNER, Gent., against
CLATER SMITH having attended Court one day, ordered that FIELDING TURNER
pay him twenty five pounds of tobacco for the same
        - MARY BOYLE, Wife of WILLIAM BOYLE, an Evidence for FIELDING
TURNER, Gent., against CLATER SMITH, having attended Court one day, ordered
that said FIELDING pay to the said WILLIAM, twenty five pounds of tobacco for the
same

p.   Loudoun County Court 14th of July 1761
481   - MARY STOKER, an Evidence for FIELDING TURNER, Gent., against
        CLATER SMITH, having attended Court one day, ordered that said
FIELDING pay her twenty five pounds of tobacco for the same
        - Upon the Petition of HENRY MOORE setting forth that the MOUNTAIN
ROAD as it now stands is very injurious to him and praying that the Road may be
turned the most convenient way, it is ordered that FIELDING TURNER, CHARLES
TYLER and FRANCIS PEYTON, Gent., or any two of them, being first sworn before
a Justice for this County, do view the most convenient way to turn the said Road and
make a report of the conveniency and inconveniency that will attend the same to the
Court

- On motion of SUSANNA GRIMES against JOHN DAVIS for detaining of her as a Servant contrary to an Order of this Court, ordered that an Attachment of Contempt issue against him returnable here at the next Court
- WILLIAM WEST, RICHARD COLEMAN and JOSIAS CLAPHAM, Gent., are by the Court recommended to the Honble. the Lieutenant Governor of this Colony for one of them to be commissioned by him to execute the Office of Sherif of this County for the ensuing year
- Ordered that the Court be adjourned till the second Tuesday in August next
- The Minutes of these Proceedings were signed

"FIELDING TURNER"

- At a Court held for Loudoun County at the Courthouse on Tuesday the Eleventh day of August one thousand seven hundred and sixty one and in the first year of the Reign of our Sovereign Lord George the Third by the grace of God of Great Britain, France and Ireland, King, Defender of the faith, &c., Before his Majesty's Justices of the Peace for the said County, to wit;

JAMES HAMILTON   JOSIAS CLAPHAM   and
RICHARD COLEMAN   BENJAMIN GRAYSON   Gent.

- Ordered that a :Licence be granted to JOHN EVANS to keep an ORDINARY at the House where WILLIAM DODD formerly lived for one year from this time, he with Security having entered into Bond as the Law directs
- Bess, a Negro girl belonging to ROGER WIGGINTON, is by the Court adjudged to be twelve years of age
- Ordered that JOHN LEWIS be appointed a CONSTABLE for this County below GOOSE CREEK

p.   Loudoun County Court 11th of August 1761
482   - A Revocation from CATESBY COCKE, Esqr. to a Letter of Attorney made
       by said CATESBY to AENEAS CAMPBELL, Gent., was proved by the Oath of JAMES HAMILTON, Gent., and by the Affirmation of GEORGE GREGG (a Quaker), witnesses thereto, and is ordered to be recorded
- Indentures of Lease and Release between JOHN TRAMMELL of the one part and WILLIAM JONES of the other part and the Receipt thereon endorsed were acknowledged by said JOHN and is ordered to be recorded
- Indentures of Lease and Release between JOHN HANBY of the one part and JOHN TRAMMELL of the other part and the Receipt thereon endorsed was acknowledged by JOHN HANBY and is ordered to be recorded
- Ordered that BENJAMIN COCKRILL be appointed a CONSTABLE for this County
- Ordered that HUGH BLACK be appointed a CONSTABLE for this County
- Indentures of Lease and Release between MARGARET SINCLEAR, Widow, of the one part and JOHN TRAMMELL of the other part and the Receipt thereon endorsed were proved by the Oaths of AARON RICHARDSON and JOHN SINCLEAR and by the Affirmation of JOHN HANBY (a Quaker) witnesses thereto and ordred to be recorded
- Indentures of Lease and Release between JOSIAS CLAPHAM, Gent., of the

one part and EVAN PRICE, Gent., of the other part and the Receipt thereon
endorsed were acknowledged by said JOSIAS and ordered to be recorded
              - Present. JOHN MUCKLEHANEY, Gent.
      - Indentures of Lease and Release between FRANCIS WILKS and MARTHA
his Wife of the one part and EDMON PHILLIPS of the other part and the Receipt
thereon endorsed were acknowledged by the said FRANCIS, and the Release was
acknowledged by the said MARTHA, she having been first privily examined as the
Law directs, and together with the Lease and Receipt ordered to be recorded
      - An Indenture of Bargain and Sale between JOSIAS CLAPHAM, Gent., of one
part and EVAN PRICE, Gent., of other part was acknowledged by the said JOSIAS
and is ordered to be recorded
      - JOHN FIELDER on his motion is discharged from the paiment of levies, &c.,
for the future
      - An Indenture of Feofment between THOMAS PRITCHARD and RACHEL
his Wife of the one part and JACOB SHILLING of the other part and the Memorandum of Livery of Seisen and Receipt thereon endorsed were acknowledged by the said
THOMAS and the Indenture and Memorandum were also acknowledged by the said
RACHEL, she having been first privily examined as the Law directs, and together
with the Receipt ordered to be recorded
      - WILLIAM OWSLEY, Plt. against JAMES ROGERS, Deft.   In Debt
Discontinued, Plt. not further prosecuting

p.   Loudoun County Court 11th of August 1761
433   - A Report of the Persons appointed to view the most convenient way for a
      Road leading from the POTOWMACK RIVER between the BLUE RIDGE and
SHORT HILLS into the Road that leads to JOHN HOUGH's Mill, was returned in
these words, vizt. "These are to acquaint the Honble. Gentlemen of the Bench that we
have upon Oath looked over and marked out a way for a Road leading from the
POTOWMACK RIVER to the MOUNTAIN ROAD between the BLUE RIDGE and
SHORT HILLS to the best of our skill and knowledge, both for good ground and con-
viency of the Inhabitants. August 8th 1761. ROBERT YELDALL, NICHOLAS
OSBORN." Whereupon it is ordered by the Court that the Road be cleared according
to the Report, that JAMES CONARD be appointed Surveyor thereof and that JOHN
MUCKLEHANEY, Gent., allot the hands to work thereon
      - WILLIAM DODD, agt. JOHN WORMSLEY   On Petition
On motion of Deft. and making Oath that JOHN WILLSON is a material witness
in this Cause and that he resides in the Province of MARYLAND, a Commission is
awarded him to examine and take the Deposition of JOHN WILLSON giving Plt. legal
notice of the time and place of executing the same
      - Indentures of Lease and Release between JOHN WEST, Gent., and CATHA-
RINE his Wife of the one part and JOHN HOUGH, Gent., of the other part and the
Receipt thereon endorsed were proved by the Oaths of FRANCIS DADE, BENJA-
MIN SEBASTIAN and STEPHEN DONALDSON, witnesses thereto, and ordered to
be recorded
      - Indenture of Lease and Release between THOMAS PLUMMER and ELLEN
his Wife of the one part and JOHN HOUGH of the other part and the Receipt thereunder written were acknowledged by said THOMAS and ELLEN, she having been

first privately examined as the Law directs, and ordered to be recorded

- Ordered that SAMUEL SMITH, WILLIAM SMITH and THOMAS STUMP or any two of them being first sworn before a Justice of this County, do view the most convenient way for a Road from THOMAS STUMP's Landing to LEESBURG and make report of the conveniency and inconveniency that will attend the same to the Court

- An Indenture of Feofment between DANIEL DAVIS and ELIZABETH his Wife of one part and JOHN CARGILL of the other part was acknowledged by the said DANIEL and ELIZABETH, she being first privily examined as the Law directs, and the Memorandum of Livery of Seisen thereon endorsed was acknowledged by the said DANIEL and together with the Indenture ordered to be recorded

- Ordered that FRANCIS HERONIMOUS build a House ten feet square to secure PALDOS HERONIMOUS, a Lunitick Person, until he recovers his reason, that he be confined therein and that THOMAS OWSLEY and WILLIAM OWSLEY go there weekly and see that he is found with all necessaries by the said FRANCIS for his support

p.   Loudoun County Court 11th of August 1761
484   - An Indenture of Feofment between SAMUEL GRIGSBY of one part and
         JAMES LANE, JUNR. of the other part and the Memorandum of Livery of Seisen thereunder written were proved by the Oath of WILLIAM JETT, JUNR., a witness thereto, and the same having been before proved by the Oaths of THOMAS CONNELL and BIRKETT JETT, witnesses thereto, ordered to be recorded

- Ordered that the Churchwardens of Cameron Parish bind out JESSE McNEAL, an Orphan, to THOMAS LEWELLING according to Law who is learn him the Trade of a Cordwainer

- WILLIAM JETT, JUNR., Quarter Master; JAMES LANE, JUNR., Captain and CHARLES ESKRIDGE, Ensign in the Militia of this County took the Oaths to his Majesty's Person and Government and subscribed the Abjuration Oath and the Test

- BRYAN ALLERSON, Plt. agt. THOMAS HAWKINS, Deft.
Upon an Attachment
Continued till the next Court for the Garnishee to declare

- The Petition of GEORGE SIMPSON against JOHN CAMBDEN is continued till next Court at motion of costs of Plt.

- Upon Petition of JOHN DAVIS against SAMPSON TURLEY for a Debt due by Account, This day came the parties by their Attornies, who being fully heard, it is considered by the Court that Plt. recover against Deft. one pound, nineteen shillings and one penny half penny and his costs by him in this behalf expended

- Upon Petition of CHRISTOPHER PERFECT against MICHAEL VAN BUSCART for a Debt due by Account, This day came Plt. by FRANCIS DADE, his Attorney and Deft. having been duly summoned was solemnly called but came not; Therefore it is considered by the Court that Plt. recover against Deft. one pound, ten shillings and his costs by him in this behalf expended

- FERDINANDO O'NEAL, Plt. agt. JOSEPH PHILLIS, Deft.   In Case
This suit is dismissed being agreed by the parties

- The Petition of WILLIAM WAITE against SAMUEL HANSON is discontinued
- The Petition of WILLIAM WAITE against THOMAS SHROSBURY is discontinued
- The Petition of ROBERT CARTER, Esqr. against ARTHUR MORTIMORE is dismissed, being agreed by the parties
- ThePetition of JOHN McGINNIS against JOSHUA GORE, JUNR. on hearing the parties, is dismissed, the Petition being brought too soon

p.   Loudoun County Court 11th of August 1761
485   - Upon Petition of WILLIAM ROSS, Admr. &c. of THOMAS EVANS, deced.
          against MARY McGEACH, Exrx. &c. of JOSEPH McGEACH, deced., for a
Debt due by a Judgment of FAIRFAX County Court; This day came Plt. by HUGH
WEST his Attorney and Deft. having been duly served with a copy of the Petition and
Summons was solemnly called but came not. Therefore it is considered by the Court
that Plt. recover against Deft. two pounds seven shillings and three pence with Interest thereon from the thirteenth day of May 1752 till the same is paid, and fifty two
pounds of nett tobacco and also his costs by him in this behalf expended to be levied of
the goods and chattels of the Decedent in the hands of the Deft. to be administered, if
so much thereof she hath, if not then the costs to be levied of her proper goods and
chattels
          - Upon Petition of JOHN HOUGH for leave to erect a Griss Mill over GOOSE
CREEK in this County near where the Main Road crosses said Creek at the Lower
Ford and to have one acre of land laid off adjacent thereto belonging to (blank) SELDON, a Report was returned by the Sherif in these words, vizt. "Pursuant to the
above Order hereunto annexed, I have summoned twelve Freeholders of my Bailiwick
who being duly sworn before AENEAS CAMPBELL, Gent., one of our Justices of our
said County, to value and appraise one acre of Land petitioned for by JOHN HOUGH
adjoining the land of the said HOUGH at GOOSE CREEK FORD, the acre of land
being laid off and bounded by GEORGE WEST, Gent., Surveyor of the said County.
We the Jurors find the acre of land to be of the value of twenty shillings current
money and the conveniences and Timber with the lands adjacent thereto that may be
laid under water by Daming for said Mill to be of the value of Eleven pounds current
money. Given under our hands and seals this 31st day of July 1761
                                        JOHN MOSS, S. Sherif

BENJAMIN EDWARDS	PHILIP COUNCH	WILLIAM BERRY
JOHN HERYFORD	THOMAS SORRELL	CORNELIUS DONOHOE
JAMES MURRAY	JOSEPH WEST	WILLIAM ROSS
JAMES ABBET	WILLIAM DODD	DANIEL MILLER

And the said JOHN HOUGH tendered in Court the sum of Twenty shillings current
money but no person appearing who was intituled to receive the same, it is ordered
that he retain the same in his hands until it be legally demanded and on the prayer of
said JOHN, it is considered that the Report be recorded and that he hold the acre of
land according to the direction of the Act of Assembly in that case made and provided
          - Upon Petition of ANDREW ADAM against WILLIAM BERKLEY for a Debt
due by Account; This day came Plt. by HUGH WEST, his Attorney, and Deft. having
been duly served with a Copy of this Petition and Summons was solemnly called but
came not. Therefore it is considered by the Court that Plaintif recover against Defen-

dant four pounds, ten shillings and six pence half penny and his costs by him in this behalf expended

p.   Loudoun County Court 11th of August 1761
486   - FRANCIS WILKS, Plt. against THOMAS GREGG, Executor, &c. of
        JOHN GREGG, deceased, Deft.   Upon an Attachment
   This day came the Plt. by HUGH WEST, his Attorney, and the Deft. came not altho' solemnly called. Therefore it is considered by the Court that Plt. recover against Deft. two pounds, three shillings and six pence and his costs by him in this behalf expended to be levied of the goods and chattels of the Testator in the hands of Deft. to be administered if so much thereof he hath, if not then the costs to be levied of his proper goods and chattels, and Deft. in mercy, &c.
   DANIEL JONES, a Garnishee in this suit being examined confesses that he has in his hands of Deft.'s Estate three pounds, eight shillings and seven pence. It is ordered that he pay the same to Plt. towards satisfying of his Judgment aforesaid.
        - Ordered that the Court be adjourned till tomorrow morning eight o'clock
        - The Minutes of these Proceedings were signed
                                        " JAMES HAMILTON "

        - At a Court continued and held for Loudoun County at the Courthouse on Wednesday the Twelfth day of August one thousand seven hundred and sixty one, Before his Majesty's Justices of the Peace for the said County, to wit;
JAMES HAMILTON   JOSIAS CLAPHAM
AENEAS CAMPBELL   CHARLES TYLER   &
             BENJAMIN GRAYSON,   Gent.

        - An Indenture of Feofment between THOMAS HALE, Son & Heir at Law of WILLIAM HALE, late of Virginia, deced., of the one part and WILLIAM WEST of the other part and the Memorandum of Livery of Seisin and Receipt thereon endorsed were acknowledged by the said THOMAS and ordered to be recorded
        - The Petition of JOSEPH JANNEY against HENRY PICKREL is dismissed being agreed
        - The Petition of BENJAMIN SEBASTIAN against WILLIAM COL-CLOUGH, Admr., &c. of ROBERT COLCLOUGH, deced., is discontinued
                - Present. RICHARD COLEMAN, Gent.
        - The Petition of PHILIP LANGFIT against SAMPSON TURLEY is continued till next Court by consent of the parties
        - The Petition of FRANCIS MOORE against LEONARD EATON is discontinued

p.   Loudoun County Court 12th of August 1761
487   - GEORGE JOHNSTON, Gent. agt. THOMAS BOTTS,   On Petition
   The Deft. being returned not found, ordered that another summons issue against him returnable here at next Court
                - Absent AENEAS CAMPBELL, Gent.
        - A Report of the Persons appointed to view the most convenient way to turn the Road petitioned for by HENRY MOORE was returned in these words, vizt., "Pur-

suant to an Order of Loudoun County Court, We the Subscribers being first sworn before JAMES LANE, Gent., have viewed the Road to us directed and find that the Road as it now stands is very inconvenient to HENRY MOORE, Gent., the Petitioner, and further that it may be turned as it is now marked by our direction which will be as good and convenient as where it now runs, as witness our hands this 10th day of August 1761. FIELDING TURNER, CHAS: TYLER, FRANCIS PEYTON." Whereupon it is ordered that said HENRY have leave to turen the Road according to the Report and that CHARLES ESKRIDGE, Surveyor of the Old Road, clear the same and keep it in repair according to Law

     - JAMES NISBET, Plt. against JAMES LEITH, Deft.   In Case

This day came the parties by their Attornies and the Jury formerly impannelled and sworn in this Cause being called and failing to appear, by consent they are discharged and thereupon came another Jury to wit;

OWEN ROBERTS	JOHN LEWIS	JOHN WINN
JOHN BISHOP	HUGH BLACK	RICHARD KEEN
ISAAC FOUCH	JOSHUA TAYLOR	JAMES WHALEY
DENNIS DALLIS	JOHN POPKINS and	JOHN SASSER

who being elected tried and sworn the truth to speak upon the issue joined, returned a Special Verdict in these words, vizt. "We the Jury sworn and impannelled to try the issue joined find for the Plt. forty shillings current money if the Law is for him, if not, We find for the Deft." And the suit is continued till the next Court for the matters of Law arising thereupon to be argued

     - Present. WILLIAM WEST, Gent.

     - An Indenture of Release between Messrs. JOHN CARLYLE and JOHN DALTON, of the one part and JOSIAS CLAPHAM of the other part was proved by the Oaths of HUGH WEST, BENJAMIN SEBASTIAN and FRANCIS DADE, witnesses thereto and is ordered to be recorded

     - CHARLES CARTER, Esqr., Executor, &c. of the Last Will and Testament of Colo. HENRY FITZHUGH, deced., Plt. against RICHARD STEPHENS, Deft. In Debt

JOSEPH STEPHENS of this County comes into Court and undertakes for Deft. that in case he shall be cast in this suit that he shall pay and satisfy the condemnation of the Court or render his body to Prison in execution for the same, or that he, the said JOSEPH, will do it for him; And Deft. saving to himself all advantages of Exceptions as well to the Plt.'s Writ as to his Declaration prays and has leave to imparl till next Court and then to plead

p. 488   <u>Loudoun County Court 12th of August 1761</u>

     - JAMES INGOE DOZER, Plt. against JAMES LEITH, Deft.   In Case

     - This day came the parties by their Attornies and thereupon came also a Jury to wit;

WILLIAM DODD	JOHN WORMSLEY	JOHN TRAMMELL, JUNR.
JOHN HERYFORD	THOMAS BRINKER	JONATHAN DAVIS
EZEKIEL HICKMAN	FRANCIS MOORE	WILLIAM OWSLEY
WILLIAM CONNELL	HUGH HINSON and	JOHN LEWIS

who being elected tried and sworn the truth to speak upon the issue joined, upon their Oath do say that Deft. did assume upon himself in manner and form as Plt. against him hath declared and they do assess Plt.'s damages by occasion of Deft.'s non performance of that assumption to five pounds, ten shillings and four pence current money and three hundred forty one pounds of tobacco besides his costs; Therefore it is considered by the Court that Plt. recover against Deft. his damages aforesaid in form aforesaid assessed and his costs by him about his suit in this behalf expended, and Deft. in mercy, &c.

     - Nan, a Negro girl belonging to JOHN LEWIS, is adjudged by the Court to be twelve years of age

     - Upon Petition of ANDREW ADAM against JOHN ROSS DEWITT for a Debt due by Account, This day came Plt. by HUGH WEST his Attorney and Deft. having been duly summoned was solemnly called but came not; Therefore it is considered by the Court that Plt. recover against Deft. four pounds, eighteen shillings and seven pence half penny and his costs in this behalf expended

     - RICHARD BARTLESON, Plt. against WILLIAM DYALL, Deft.
     Upon an Attachment
This day came Plt. by HUGH WEST, his Attorney, and Deft. came not altho' solemnly called. Therefore it is considered by the Court that Plt. recover against Deft. three pounds, fifteen shillings and his costs by him in this behalf expended and Deft. in mercy, &c.

     - HUGH BLACK, Plt. against LEVY LEWIS, Deft.
     Upon an Attachment
Discontinued, the Plt. not further prosecuting

     - Upon Petition of FRANKLIN PERRY against MARGARET JENKINS, Admrx., &c. of SAMUEL JENKINS, deced., for a Debt due by Account, This day cam Plt. by HUGH WEST, his Attorney, and Deft. having been duly summonmed was solomnly called but came not; Therefore it is considered by the Court that Plt. recover against Deft. eight hundred pounds of crop tobacco and his costs by him in this behalf expended, to be levied of the goods and chattels of the said Intestate which shall hereafter come to the hands of Deft. to be administered

p.   <u>Loudoun County Court 12th of August 1761</u>
489   - JAMES DOZER, an Evidence of JAMES INGOE DOZER against JAMES
     LEITH having attended Court two daies, and for travelling thirty miles from FAIRFAX County and returning, ordered that the said JAMES INGOE pay him one hundred forty pounds of tobacco for the same

     - Absent. RICHARD COLEMAN, Gent.

     - RICHARD COLEMAN, Gent., Plt. against OWEN ROBERTS, Deft.
     In Trespass
    This day came the parties by their Attornies and thereupon came also a Jury, to wit;

JOHN SASSER	JOSEPH STEPHENS	JOSHUA GORE
JOHN LEWIS	WILLIAM OWSLEY	FRANCIS MOORE
THOMAS BRINKER	RICHARD KEEN	JAMES DOZER
JOHN HERYFORD	JOHN THOMAS and	JOHN TRAMMELL

who being elected tried and sworn the truth to speak upon the issue joined, pon their Oath do say that Deft. is Guilty in manner and form as Plt. against them hath declared and they do assess Plt.'s damages by occasion thereof to twenty shillings current money. Therefore it is considered by the Court that Plt. recover against Deft. his damages aforesaid in form aforesaid assessed and twenty shillings for his costs by him about his suit in this behalf expended and the Deft. in mercy, &c.

     - Present. RICHARD COLEMAN, Gent.

- WILLIAM DODD, Plt. agt. GEORGE HEADEN, Deft.

Upon an Attachment

This day came Plt. by HUGH WEST, his Attorney, and Deft. came not altho' solemnly called. Therefore it is considered by the Court that Plt. recover against Deft. eighteen shillings and six pence and also his costs by him in this behalf expended, and the Deft. in mercy, &c.

JAMES VESSELS, a Garnishee being sworn declared that he has nothing of the Deft. in his hands and thereupon he is discharged. JOHN McCARTY, a Garnishee, also sworn declares he has in his hands of Deft.'s effects five and a half yards of German Serge and an half yard of shaloon, one an an half yards of sheeting Linnen and half yard of Buckrum. It is ordered that said JOHN deliver the goods to the Sherif and that he sell the same according to Law and out of the money arising from such sale pay and satisfy Plt.'s Debt and costs aforesaid if they sell for so much and render the overplus if any to the Deft.

- Indentures of Lease and Release between JOSIAS CLAPHAM, Gent. of the one part and ROBERT POPKINS of the other part and the Receipt thereon endorsed were acknowledged by the said JOSIAS and ordered to be recorded

- Indentures of Lease and Release between JOSIAS CLAPHAM, Gent. of the one part and JOHN POPKINS of the other part and the Receipt thereon endorsed were acknowledged by the said JOSIAS and ordered to be recorded

- The Petition of JAMES KENNERLY, Assignee of ELIZABETH VICK, against BENJAMIN GRAYSON, Gent., is continued till next Court by consent of the parties

- Upon Petition of JAMES INGOE DOZER against WILLIAM FIELDER for a Debt due by Note of Hand, This day came the parties by their Attornies and being fully heard, it is considered by the Court that Plt. recover against Deft. four pounds, eight shillings and three pence three farthings and his costs by him in this behalf expended, including seven shillings and six pence for a Lawyer's fee

p.   Loudoun County Court 12th of August 1761
490   - Upon Petition of JAMES BOGGESS against JAMES SPENCER for a
        Debt due by Account, This day came Plt. by FRANCIS DADE, his Attorney, and Deft. having been duly served with a copy of the Petition and Summons was solemnly called but came not. Therefore it is considered by the Court that Plt. recover against Deft. four pounds, nineteen shillings and eleven pence three farthings and his costs by him in this behalf expended

- BENJAMIN GRAYSON and CRAVEN PEYTON, Plts. against
WILLIAM FIELDER, otherwise called WILLIAM FIELDER of Loudoun
County, Deft.   In Debt

JOSHUA TAYLOR of this County comes into Court and undertakes for Deft. that in case he shall be cast in this suit that he will pay and satisfy the condemnation of the Court or render his body to Prison in execution for the same, or that he, the said JOSHUA, will do it for him. And Deft. saving to himself all advantages of Exceptions as well to Plt.'s Writ as to his Declaration, prays and has leave to imparl till next Court and then to plead

- Upon Petition of JOSIAS CLAPHAM, Gent., agaisnt THOMAS AWBREY for a Debt due by Account, This day came Plt. in his proper person and Deft. having been duly summoned was solemnly called but came not; Therefore it is considered by the Court that Plt. recover against Deft. one pound, twelve shillings and six pence and his costs by him in this behalf expended

      - Absent. CHARLES TYLER, Gent.

      - JOHN TRAMMELL, Plt. against WILLIAM COLVIN, Deft.

Upon an Attachment

Discontinued, Plt. not further prosecuting

      - JOSIAS CLAPHAM, Plt. against WILLIAM COLVIN, Deft.

Upon an Attachment

This day came Plt. by WILLIAM ELLZEY his Attorney and Deft. came not altho' solemnly called. Therefore it is considered by the Court that Plt. recover against Deft. sixteen pounds, one shilling nd five pence and his costs by him in this behalf expended and the Deft. in mercy, &c.

The Sherif having returned that he had levied the Attachment on two hogsheads of tobacco and two horses and a Mare and Colt, it is ordered that he sell the same according to Law and out of the money arising from such sale pay and satisfy Plt. his Debt and costs aforesaid if they sell for so much and render the overplus if any to the Deft.

      - WILLIAM WEST, JUNR. Plt. agt. ISAAC FORESTER, Deft.   In Case

Discontinued, Plt. not further prosecuting

p. 491   **Loudoun County Court 12th of August 1761**

      - JAMES HOOK, Plt. agt. WILLIAM COLVIN, Deft. Upon an Attachment Continued till next Court at motion and costs of Plt.

      - Ordered that the Court be adjourned till the second Tuesday in September next

      - The Minutes of these Proceedings were signed

                        " JAS: HAMILTON "

      - At a Court held for Loudoun County at the Courthouse on Tuesday the Eighth day of September in the first year of the Reign of our Sovereign Lord George the Third by the grace of God of Great Britain France and Ireland, King, Defender of the faith, &c., Anno Domini one thousand seven hundred and sixty one, Before his Majesty's Justices of the Peace for the said County, to wit;

FRANCIS LIGHTFOOT LEE   BENJAMIN GRAYSON &

AENEAS CAMPBELL   JOHN MUCKLEHANEY,   Gent.

      - A Commission from the Honble. the Lieutenant Governor to WILLIAM WEST, Esqr., to be SHERIFF of this County during pleasure was produced in Court by the said WILLIAM and thereupon together with JAMES HAMILTON, NICHOLAS MINOR, RICHARD COLEMAN and HUGH WEST, Gent., his Securities, entered into and acknowledged their Bonds for the said WILLIAM's due performance of his Office and for collecting Fines, &c., and also for collecting the Land and Poll Tax which are ordered to be recorded; And then said WILLIAM took and subscribed the usual Oaths to his Majesty's Person and Government and subscribed the Test and also took the Oath of SHERIFF of this County and the Oath appointed by the Tobacco Law

      - Present. JAMES HAMILTON & RICHARD COLEMAN, Gent.

- WILLIAM WEST, JUNR., JOHN MOSS, JUNR., and JOHN MINOR having taken the usual Oaths to his Majesty's Person and Government and subscribed the Abjuration Oath and Test were on motion of WILLIAM WEST, Gent., Sheriff of this County sworn and admitted his UNDER SHERIFF's and then WILLIAM WEST, JUNR., JOHN MOSS, JUNR., and JOHN MINOR took the Oath appointed by the Tobacco Law
    - Cate, a Negro girl belonging to WILLIAM NODING, is adjudged by the Court to be thirteen years of age
    - Ordered that JOHN WARFORD be added to the List of Tithables taken for this County this present year

p.   Loudoun County Court 8th of September 1761
492   - Ordered that THOMAS BRYAN be added to the List of Tithables taken for this County this present year
    - Ordered that EPHRAIM DUNHAM be added to the List of Tithables taken for this County this present year
    - Ordered that NEHEMIAH GARRISON and his three Tithables, to wit, MOSES GARRISON, AARON GARRISON and JOHN GARRISON, be added to the List of Tithables taken for this County this present year
    - Ordered that WILLIAM SHREIVE be added to the List of Tithables taken for this County this present year
    - An Indenture of Gift between WILLIAM WEST, Gent., of the one part and CRAVEN PEYTON, Mercht., Son in Law of WILLIAM WEST, of the other part; and the Memorandum of Livery of Seisin thereon endorsed were acknowledged by the said WILLIAM and ordered to be recorded
    - Indentures of Lease and Release between FRANCIS HAGUE and JANE his Wife of the one part and AENEAS CAMPBELL, Gent., of the other part and the Receipt thereon endorsed were proved by the Oaths of NICHOLAS MINOR, Gent., WILLIAM BAKER and CHRISTOPHER PERFECT, witnesses thereto, and ordered to be recorded
    - Indentures of Lease and Release between ANDREW LINK of the one part and AENEAS CAMPBELL, Gent., of the other part and the Receipt thereon endorsed were proved by the Oaths of NICHOLAS MINOR, Gent., JOHN URQUHART and by the Affirmation of JOSEPH JANNEY (a Quaker) the witnesses thereto, and ordered to be recorded
    - Indentures of Lease and Release between FRANCIS HAGUE and JANE his Wife of the one part and AENEAS CAMPBELL, Gent. of the other part and the Receipt thereon endorsed were proved by the Oaths of NICHOLAS MINOR, Gent., WILLIAM BAKER and CHRISTOPHER PERFECT witnesses thereto and ordered to be recorded
    - An Indenture of Lease for Lives between JOHN CARLYLE, Gent., Attorney in Fact for GEORGE WILLIAM FAIRFAX, Esqr., of the one part and BENJAMIN DAVIS of the other part, was acknowledged by the said JOHN and is ordered to be recorded
    - An Indenture of Lease for Lives between JOHN CARLYLE, Gent., Attorney in Fact for GEORGE WILLIAM FAIRFAX, Esqr., of the one part and JOHN BUTCHER of the other part was acknowledged by the said JOHN and is ordered to

be recorded
- An Indenture of Lease for Lives between JOHN CARLYLE, Gent., Attorney
in Fact for GEORGE WILLIAM FAIRFAX, Esqr., of the one part and GEORGE
FOUT of the other part was acknowledged by JOHN CARLYLE and is ordered to be
recorded

p.   Loudoun County Court 8th of September 1761
493   - An Indenture of Lease for Lives between JOHN CARLYLE, Gent., Attorney
       in Fact for GEORGE WILLIAM FAIRFAX, Esqr., of the one part and JOHN
HAVEN of the other part was acknowledged by the said JOHN and is ordered to be
recorded
       - An Indenture of Lease for Lives between JOHN CARLYLE, Gent., Attorney
in Fact for GEORGE WILLIAM FAIRFAX, Esqr., of the one part and ROBERT
YELDING of the other part was acknowledged by JOHN CARLYLE and is ordered to
be recorded
       - An Indenture of Surrender of Lands from ANN MASON, Widow, to THOM-
SON MASON was proved by the Oaths of EVAN WILLIAMS and PHILIP SULLI-
VAN, witnesses thereto
       - Ordered that JOHN MUCKLEHANEY, Gent., allot the hands to work on the
Road whereof JOHN OSBORN is Surveyor
       - NICHOLAS MINOR, Gent., named in the Commission of the Peace for this
County, took the usual Oaths to his Majesty's Person and Government and took and
subscribed the Abjuration Oath and subscribed the Test, and also took the Oath of a
Justice of the Peace and of the County Court in Chancery
              - Present. NICHOLAS MINOR, Gent.
       - Indentures of Lease and Release between CHARLES GREEN, Clerk,
Minister of Truro Parish, and MARGARET his Wife of the one part and WILLIAM
ELLZEY of the other part and the Receipt thereunder written, also a Bond for perfor-
mance of Covenants from CHARLES GREEN to WILLIAM ELLZEY were acknow-
ledged by the Oaths of THOMAS BLACKBURN, THOMAS EWELL and JOHN
HANCOCK, witnesses thereto, and ordered to be recorded

p.   Loudoun County Court 8th of September 1761
494   - An Indenture of Feofment between NICHOLAS MINOR of the one part
       and MICHAEL LEATHERMAN of the other part and the Memorandum of
Livery of Seisin thereon endorsed were acknowledged by said NICHOLAS and ordered
to be recorded
       - Ordered that the Churchwardens of Cameron Parish bind out JOHN WINN
HAYS, being three years old the first day of May last past, to JOHN HALL according
to Law
       - JOHN MOSS, an Evidence for JAMES NISBET against JAMES LEITH
having attended Court seven daies, ordered that JAMES NISBET pay him one hundred seventy five pounds of tobacco for the same
       - ROBERT WOOD, an Evidence for JAMES LEITH at the suit of JAMES
NISBET, having attended Court seven daies, ordered that JAMES LEITH pay him
one hundred seventy five pounds of tobacco for the same

- BRYAN ALLERSON, Plt. aglt. THOMAS HAWKINS, Deft.
   Upon an Attachment
This day came Plt. by HUGH WEST, his Attorney, and Deft. came not altho'
solemnly called. Therefore it is considered by the Court that Plt. recover against Deft.
ten pounds, one shilling and seven pence half penny and his costs by him in this behalf expended and the Deft. in mercy, &c.
   WILLIAM LITTLETON, a Garnishee, being sworn declares that he has in his
hands of Deft.'s effects eight hundred fifty five pounds of transfer tobacco which said
WILLIAM delivered to Plt.'s Attorney, the Court rating the same at fourteen shillings
p ct. and it is also ordered that Plt. receive the same at that rate in part satisfaction
of his Debt and costs aforesaid
   - Indentures of Lease and Release between MARY ANSLEY of the one part
and CRAVEN PEYTON, Gent., of other part and Receipt thereon endorsed were acknowledged by said MARY and ordered to be recorded
   - Indentures of Lease and Release between JOSEPH WEST of the one part
and JOHN QUEEN of the other part and the Receipt thereon endorsed were acknowledged by said JOSEPH and ordered to be recorded
   - An Indenture of Lease for Lives between JOHN CARLYLE, Gent., Attorney
in Fact for GEORGE WILLIAM FAIRFAX, Esqr. of the one part and SIMON SHO-
MAKER of the other part was acknowledged by said JOHN and ordered to be
recorded
   - Ordered that PATRICK MOLHOLLAND be added to the List of Tithables
taken for this County this present year

p.   Loudoun County Court 8th of September 1761
495   - WILLIAM JETT, JUNR., Plt. agt. JOSEPH SOLE, Deft.
   Upon an Attachment
This day came Plt. in his proper person and Deft. came not alth' solemnly called;
Therefore it is considered by the Court that Plt. recover against Deft. three pounds,
two shillings and two pence and his costs by him in this behalf expended, and Deft. in
mercy, &c.
   JACOB REMEY, JUNR., a Garnishee, being sworn declares that he has in his
hands of Deft.'s effects one pound, ten shillings and ten pence. It is ordered that he
pay the same to Plt. towards satisfying of his Debt and costs aforesaid
   - Upon Petition of ANTHONY RUSSELL, Gent., against ROBERT WOOD for
a Debt due by Account, This day came the parties in their proper persons and Deft.
acknowledged Plt.'s action to be just. Therefore it is considered by the Court that Plt.
recover against Deft. three pounds, two shillings, his Debt due as aforesaid, and his
costs by him in this behalf expended
   - An Indenture of Lease for Lives between JOHN CARLYLE, Gent., Attorney
in Fact for GEORGE WILLIAM FAIRFAX, Esqr. of the one part and PETER SHO-
MAKER of the other part was acknowledged by said JOHN and ordered to be
recorded
   - An Indenture of Lease for Lives between JOHN CARLYLE, Gent., Attorney
in Fact for GEORGE WILLIAM FAIRFAX, Esqr., of the one part and GEORGE
SHOMAKER of the other part was acknowledged by the said JOHN and ordered to be
recorded

- An Indenture of Lease for Lives between JOHN CARLYLE, Gent., Attorney in Fact for GEORGE WILLIAM FAIRFAX, Esqr. of the one part and ADAM WINSALL of the other part was acknowledged by the said JOHN and is ordered to be recorded

- An Indenture of Lease for Lives between JOHN CARLYLE, Gent., Attorney in Fact for GEORGE WILLIAM FAIRFAX, Esqr. of the one part and FRANCIS BALDWIN of the other part was acknowledged by the said JOHN and is ordered to be recorded

- An Indenture of Lease for Lives between JOHN CARLYLE, Gent., Attorney in Fact for GEORGE WILLIAM FAIRFAX, Esqr. of the one part and JAMES ROSS of the other part, was acknowledged by the said JOHN and ordered to be recorded

- JOSHUA GORE, Plt. agt. JEREMIAH THOMAS, Deft.   In Debt
THOMAS LEWIS of this County comes into Court and undertakes for Deft. that in case he shall be cast in this suit he will pay and satisfy the condemnation of the Court or render his body to Prison in execution for the same, or that he, said THOMAS, will do it for him. And Deft. by HUGH WEST, his Attorney, saving to himself all advantages of Exceptions as well to Plt.'s Writ as to his Declaration, prays and has leave to imparl till next Court and then to plead

p.   Loudoun County Court 8th of September 1761
496   - An Indenture of Lease for Lives between JOHN CARLYLE, Gent., Attorney in Fact for GEORGE WILLIAM FAIRFAX, Esqr., of the one part and JOHN GRANT of the other part was acknowledged by JOHN CARLYLE and ordered to be recorded

- An Indenture of Lease for Lives between JOHN CARLYLE, Gent., Attorney in Fact for GEORGE WILLIAM FAIRFAX, Esqr., of the one part and WILLIAM HURLEY of the other part was acknowledged by said JOHN and is ordered to be recorded

- Indentures of Lease and Release between JOSEPH WEST of the one part and EDWARD TANNER of the other part and the Receipt thereon endorsed were acknowledged by said JOSEPH and ordered to be recorded

- Ordered that GREENBURY DORSEY and his two Tithables, to wit, Negroes Peter & Phebe, be added to the List of Tithables taken for this County this present year

- Indentures of Lease and Release between THOMAS PHILIPS and ANN his Wife of the one part and PHILIP NOLAND of the other part and the Receipt thereon endorsed were acknowledged by said THOMAS and the Release was acknowledged by said ANN, she having been first privily examined as the Law directs, and together with the Lease and Receipt ordered to be recorded

- Ordered that the Court be adjourned till tomorrow morning eight o'clock
- The Minutes of these Proceedings were signed
                              " FRANCIS LIGHTFOOT LEE "

- At a Court continued and held for Loudoun County at the Courthouse on Wednesday the Ninth day of September one thousand seven hundred and sixty one , Before his Majesty's Justices of the Peace for the said County, to wit
FIELDING TURNER   FRANCIS PEYTON   and

CHARLES TYLER   JOHN MUCKLEHANEY,   Gent.

- THOMAS HARRISON, JAMES NISBET, BENJAMIN GRAYSON and SPENCE GRAYSON, Executors, &c., of the Last Will and Testament of BENJAMIN GRAYSON, Gent., deceased, Plts. against GEORGE HANCOCK Deft.   In Case

By Consent of the parties, the Order for Arbitration in this Cause is discontinued and the suit is continued till next Court

p. **Loudoun County Court 9th of September 1761**
497   - AENEAS CAMPBELL, Gent., Plt. against DAVID DAVIS, Deft. In Case

By agreement of the parties, this suit is dismissed and it is ordered that Deft. pay unto Plt. his costs

- CHARLES TYLER, an Evidence for JAMES NISBET against JAMES LEITH, having attended Court six daies, ordered that JAMES NISBET pay him one hundred fifty pounds of tobacco for the same

- THOMAS HARRISON, JAMES NISBET, BENJAMIN GRAYSON and SPENCE GRAYSON, Executors, &c., of the Last Will and Testament of BENJAMIN GRAYSON, Gent., deceased, Plts. against THOMAS LEWELLEN, Deft.   In Case

Continued till next Court for return of the Award

- DAVID DAVIS, Plt. against HUGH FOUCH, Deft.   In Trespass

Continued till next Court at motion and costs of Plt.

- Present. AENEAS CAMPBELL & NICHOLAS MINOR, Gent.

- JOHN DAVIS, Plt. against ELIZABETH LEWIS, Deft. In Case

Continued till next Court at the motion and costs of Deft. and a Commission is awarded her to examined and take the Depositions of her witnesses in this suit, giving Plt. legal notice of the time and place of executing the same

- An Indenture of Feofment between MICHAEL STOKER and BARBARY his wife of the one part and JOHN PATTERSON of the other part and the Memorandum of Livery of Seisen thereon endorsed was acknowledged by the said MICHAEL and BARBARY, she having been first privily examined as the Law directs, and ordered to be recorded

- JOHN TARPLEY, Plt. against WILLIAM TILLERY, Deft.   In Case

This day came Plt. by his Attorney and thereupon a Jury, to wit

EZEKIEL HICKMAN	BENJAMIN MASON	JAMES MELVIN
BENJAMIN BERKLEY	ROBERT SANDFORD	THOMAS LEWIS
JOSHUA GORE	CHARLES CHILTON	ANDREW ADAM
GEORGE SIMPSON	WILLIAM BAKER and	THOMAS PRITCHARD

who being elected tried and sworn well and truly to inquire of damages in this suit, upon their Oaths do say that Plt. hath sustained damages by occasion of Deft.'s Breach of the Promise and Assumption inthe Declaration specified to eleven pounds, five shillings and nine pence three farthings besides his costs. Therefore it is considered by the Court that Plt. recover against Deft. and WILLIAM

p. **Loudoun County Court 9th of September 1761**
498   LEWIS, was was returned Security for the appearance of Deft. his damages aforesaid in form aforesaid assessed and his costs by him in this behalf ex-

pended, and the Deft. in mercy, &c.

    - An Indenture of Feofment between NICHOLAS MINOR of one part and JOHN HERYFORD of other part and the Memorandum of Livery of Seisen thereon endorsed were acknowledged by said NICHOLAS and ordered to be recorded

    - An Indenture of Feofment between BERNARD WREN and CATHARINE his Wife of the one part and JOHN MEGINNIS of the other part and the Memorandum of Livery of Seisen thereon endorsed were acknowledged by said BERNARD and CATHARINE, she having been first privily examined as the Law directs, and ordered to be recorded

    - WILLIAM MURPHEY, Plt. agt. THOMAS KELLEY, Deft.   In Case
  This day came the parties by their Attornies and thereupon came also a Jury to wit;

BENJAMIN MASON	WILLIAM BAKER	BENJAMIN EDWARDS
BENJAMIN BERKLEY	ROBERT SANDFORD	THOMAS PRITCHARD
JOSHUA GORE	EZEKIEL HICKMAN	THOMAS LEWIS
BENNETT HILL	ANDREW ADAM and	GEORGE SIMPSON

who being elected tried and sworn the truth to speak upon the issue joined in this suit, upon their Oath do say that Deft. is Guilty in manner and form as Plt. against him hath declared and they do assess Plt.'s damages by occasion thereof to two pounds besides his costs; Therefore it is considered by the Court that Plt. recover against Deft. his damages aforesaid in manner aforesaid assessed and his costs by him about his suit in this behalf expended, and Deft. in mercy, &c.

    - An Indenture of Lease for Lives between JOHN PATTERSON, Gent., and Attorney in Fact for the Right Honble. CHARLES EARL of TANKERVILLE, of one part and WILLIAM GRANT of other part, was acknowledged by JOHN PATTERSON and is ordered to be recorded

    - An Indenture of Lease for Lives between JOHN PATTERSON, Gent., and Attorney in Fact for the Right Honble. CHARLES EARL of TANKERVILLE of one part and SAMUEL COOMBS of other part was acknowledged by JOHN PATTERSON and is ordered to be recorded

    - An Indenture of Lease for Lives between JOHN PATTERSON, Gent., and Attorney in Fact for the Right Honble. CHARLES EARL of TANKERVILLE, of one part and RALPH BRADDOCK of other part was acknowledged by JOHN PATTERSON and is ordered to be recorded

    - The Petition of JAMES KENNERLY, Assignee of ELIZABETH VICK, against BENJAMIN GRAYSON, Gent., is continued till next Court by consent of parties

p.   <u>Loudoun County Court 9th of September 1761</u>
499   - An Indenture of Lease for Lives between JOHN PATTERSON, Gent., and Attorney in Fact for the Right Honble, CHARLES EARL of TANKERVILLE of one part and WILLIAM BRADDOCK of other part was acknowledged by JOHN PATTERSON and is ordered to be recorded

    - An Indenture of Lease for Lives between JOHN PATTERSON, Gent., and Attorney in Fact for the Right Honble. CHARLES EARL of TANKERVILLE of one part and JAMES FERGUSON of other part was acknowledged by JOHN PATTERSON and is ordered to be recorded

    - An Indenture of Lease for Lives between JOHN PATTERSON, Gent., and Attorney in Fact for the Right Honble. CHARLES EARL of TANKRVILLE of one part and SAMUEL SCHOOLEY of other part was acknowledged by JOHN PATTERSON and is ordered to be recorded

- An Indenture of Lease for Lives between JOHN PATTERSON, Gent., and Attorney in Fact for the Right Honble, CHARLES EARL of TANKERVILLE of one part and SAMUEL SCHOOLEY of other part was acknowledged by JOHN PATTERSON and is ordered to be recorded

- PHILIP LANGFIT, Plt. agt. SAMPSON TURLEY, Deft.   On Petition
The parties by their Attornies mutually submit all matters and accounts in difference between them to the final determination of JOHN WEST, Gent., and agree that his award thereupon to be made the Judgment of the Court and the same is ordered accordingly

- Upon Petition of GEORGE JOHNSTON, Gent. against THOMAS BOTTS for a Debt due by Account, This day came Plt. by HUGH WEST, his Attorney, and Deft. having been duly summoned and solemnly called came not; Therefore it is considered by the Court that Plt. recover against Deft. one pound, ten shilllings and seven pence and his costs by him in this behalf expended, including seven shillings and six pence for a Lawyer's fee

- Upon Petition of ARTHUR MORTIMORE against WILLIAM DYE for a Debt due by Note of Hand, This day came Plt. by BENJAMIN SEBASTIAN, his Attorney, and Deft having been duly served with a copy of the Petition and Summons was solemnly called but came not. Therefore it is considered by the Court that Plt. recover against Deft. four pounds, his Debt as aforesaid, and his costs by him in this behalf expended, including seven shillings and six pence for a Lawyer's fee

- Upon Petition of ANTHONY RUSSELL, Gent., against MOSES HALL for a Debt due by Account, This day came Plt. in lhis proper person and Deft. having been duly summoned was solemnly called but came not. Therefore it is considered by the Court that Plt. recover against Deft. two pounds fourteen shillings and four pence half penny and his costs by him in this behalf expended

- ROBERT MITCHELL, Plt. agt. ISRAEL THOMPSON, Deft. On Petition
WILLIAM ELLZEY, Gent. in Court undertakes for Plt. that in case he shall be cast

p.   Loudoun County Court 9th of September 1761
500   in this suit he shall pay and satisfy all such damages, costs and charges as
         shall be awarded against him or that he, the said WILLIAM, will do it for him;
And by consent of the parties, the Petition is continued till next Court

- The Petition of HOLLAND MIDDLETON against JOHN PHILLIPS is continued till next Court at motion and costs of Plt.

- Upon Petition of BENJAMIN SEBASTIAN against THOMAS AWBREY for a Debt due by Note of Hand; This day came Plt. in his proper person and Deft. having been duly served with a copy of the Petition and Summons was solemnly called but came not; Therefore it is considered by the Court that Plt. recover against Deft. two pounds, five shillings and one penny three farthings, his Debt as aforesaid, and his costs by him in this behalf expended

- The Petition of WILLIAM ELLZEY against DANIEL NEALE is discontinued

- The Petition of WILLIAM ELLZEY against HUGH CALDWELL is dismissed being agreed by the parties and it is ordered that Deft. pay Plt. his costs

- The Petition of CLATER SMITH against WILLIAM WEST, JUNR., on hearing the parties by their Attornies is dismissed

- The Petition of GEORGE SIMPSON against JOHN CAMBDEN on hearing the parties by their Attornies is dismissed

- HENRY WISHEART, an Evidence for GEORGE SIMPSON against JOHN CAMBDEN having attended Court two daies, ordered that said GEORGE pay him fifty pounds of tobacco for the same

- JOHN ROBINSON, an Evidence for GEORGE SIMPSON against JOHN CAMBDEN having attended Court three daies and for travelling thirty five miles from FAIRFAX County and returning three times, ordered that said GEORGE pay him three hundred ninety pounds of tobacco for the same

- BENJAMIN BERKLEY, an Evidence for GEORGE SIMPSON against JOHN CAMBDEN having attended Court four daies and travelling twenty seven miles from FAIRFAX County and returning four times, ordered that said GEORGE pay him four hundred twenty four pounds of tobacco for the same

- Indentures of Lease and Release between WILLIAM BERRY and REBEC-CA his Wife of one part and JACOB PHAW of other part was acknowledged by said WILLIAM and REBECCA, she having been first privily examined as the Law directs and the Receipt thereon endorsed was acknowledged by said WILLIAM and together with the Indentures ordered to be recorded

- Ordered that CORNELIUS DONOHOE be added to the List of Tithables taken for this County this present year

p.   Loudoun County Court 9th of September 1761
501   - Ordered that HUGH CALDWELL and his two Tithables, to wit, WILLIAM CALDWELL and HUGH CALDWELL be added to the List of Tithables taken for this County this present year

- Ordered that JOHN McCOLLOM and his Tithable, to wit, JAMES JOICE, be added to the List of Tithables for this County this present year

- JOSIAS CLAPHAM, Gent., Plt. agt. BRYAN ALLERSON, Deft. In Case WILLIAM STARKS of this County comes into Court and undertakes for Deft. that in case he shall be cast in this suit he shall pay and satisfy the condemnation of the Court or render his body to Prison in execution for the same, or that he, the said WILLIAM, will do it for him; And Deft in his proper person saving to himself all advantages of Exceptions as well to Plt.'s Writ as to his Declaration, prays and has leave to imparl till next Court and then to plead

- Ordered that JOHN WORMSLEY be added to the List of Tithables taken for this County this present year

- Upon Petition of ANTHONY RUSSELL, Gent., against JOHN DAVIS for a Debt due by Account, This day came the parties in their proper person who being fully heard, it is considered by the Court that Plt. recover against Deft. four pounds, sixteen shillings and two pence half penny and his costs by him in this behalf expended

- GEORGE CHILTON an Evidence for WILLIAM MURPHEY against THO-MAS KELLEY having attended Court three daies and travelling thirty miles from PRINCE WILLIAM County and returning twice, ordered that said WILLIAM pay him two hundred fifty five pounds of tobacco for the same

- WILLIAM HARDY an Evidence for WILLIAM MURPHEY against THO-

MAS KELLEY having attended Court two daies, ordered that WILLIAM MURPHEY pay him fifty pounds of tobacco for the same

- JAMES LEITH an Evidence for WILLIAM MURPHEY against THOMAS KELLEY having attended Court four daies, ordered that said WILLIAM pay him one hundred pounds of tobacco for the same

- THOMAS BULLITT, Plt. agt. CHARLES LEWIS, Deft.   In Case
Continued till next Court at motion and costs of Plt.

- JAMES LEITH an Evidence for ANTHONY RUSSELL, Gent., against JOHN DAVIS, having attended Court one day, ordered that said ANTHONY pay him twenty five pounds of tobacco for the same

- HENRY PEYTON, Gent., Plt. agt. SAMUEL STILLWELL, Deft. In Case
Continued till next Cort at costs of Defendant and on motion of Plt. a Commission is awarded him to examine and take the Deposition of WILLIAM SPEAKMAN, an aged

p.   Loudoun County Court 9th of September 1761
502   and infirm witness in this suit, giving Deft. legal notice of the time and place of executing the same

- WILLIAM SPEAKMAN, an Evidence for HENRY PEYTON, Gent., against SAMUEL STILLWELL having attended Court two daies and for travelling thirty miles from PRINCE WILLIAM County and returning, ordered that said SAMUEL pay him one hundred forty pounds of tobacco for the same, the Cause being continued till next Court at his costs

- LEVEN POWELL, an Evidence for HENRY PEYTON, Gent. against SAMUEL STILLWELL, having attended Court two daies and for travelling thirty miles from PRINCE WILLIAM County and returning, ordered that said SAMUEL pay him one hundred forty pounds of tobacco for the same, the Cause being continued till next Court at his costs

- JOHN CHAMP, an Evidence for HENRY PEYTON, Gent., against SAMUEL STILLWELL having attended Court two daies, ordered that said SAMUEL pay him fifty pounds of tobacco for the same, the Cause being continued till next Court at his costs

- The Petition of THOMPSON MASON, Esqr., against BENJAMIN MASON is continued till the next Court at motion and costs of Plt.

- JOSEPH MAYSE, Plt. agt. BENJAMIN GRAYSON, otherwise called I BENJAMIN GRAYSON of SPOTSYLVANIA County, Deft.   In Debt
This day came the parties by their Attornies and Deft. relinquishing his former Plea saith he cannot gainsay Plt.'s action. Therefore it is considered by the Court that Plt. recover against Deft. twenty pounds current money of Virginia, the Debt in the Declaration mentioned, and his costs by him in this behalf expended, and Deft. in mercy, &c.

- ARCHIBALD CAMPBELL, Clerk, Plt. agt. JOHN ANDREWS otherwise called I JOHN ANDREWS of the Parish of Cameron and County of FAIRFAX, Clerk, Deft.   In Debt
Continued till next Court at motion and costs of Plt.

- ALEXANDER BROWN & COMPANY, Plts. agt. JOSIAS CLAPHAM, Deft.   In Case
Continued till next Court at motion and costs of Plt.

- ALEXANDER FARROW, Plt. agt. RICHARD FREEMAN and ELIZA-
BETH FREEMAN, Defts.   In Case
Continued till next Court by consent of the parties

p.   Loudoun County Court 9th of September 1761
503   - ROBERT EASTHAM, Plt. agt. THOMAS BOTTS, Deft.   In Debt
This day came the parties by their Attornies and Deft. relinquishing his former
Plea saith he cannot gainsay Plt.'s action. Therefore it is considered by the Court
that Plt. recover against Deft. nine pounds, nineteen shillings and six pence half
penny current money of Virginia, the Debt in the Declaration mentioned and his costs
by him in this behalf expended, and the Deft. in mercy, &c.
        - JAMES INGOE DOZER, Plt. against JAMES GOULDING, Deft. In Case
This day came the parties by their Attornies and thereupon came also a Jury, to
wit;   JOHN TRAMMELL   JOHN SHEPHERD   JOSEPH HUTCHISON
        HUGH CALDWELL   JAMES SAUNDERS   CHARLES CHILTON
        GEORGE CHILTON   JOHN HALL   HENRY TAYLOR
        THOMAS LEWIS   JOHN ELLIOTT   and   ABRAHAM WEAVER
who being elected tried and sworn the truth to speak upon the issue joined, upon their
Oath do day that Deft. is Guilty in manner and form as Plt. against him hath complained and they do assess Plt.'s damages by occasion thereof to one shillings, Therefore it is considered by the Court that Plt. recover against Deft. his damages aforesaid
in form aforesaid assessed
        - JAMES MORE, Plt. agt. JOHN WALMSLEY, Deft.   In Debt
WILLIAM BERRY, JOHN McCOLLOM and THOMAS HAMILTON came into
Court and undertake for the Deft. in case he shall be cast in this suit that he will pay
and satisfy the condemnation of the Court or render his body to Prison in execution
for the same, or that they, the said WILLIAM BERRY, JOHN McCOLLOM and
THOMAS HAMILTON will do it for him; And Deft. by WILLIAM ELLZEY his Attorney, prays Oyer of the Writing Obligatory which is granted him
        CHARLES BINNS here in Court undertakes for Plt. that in case he shall be cast in
this suit that he shall pay and satisfy all such damages and costs and charges as
shall be awarded against him or that he will pay them for him
        - WILLIAM WEST, Sheriff, protested the sufficiency of the Goal built for this
County for that it is not sufficient to confine those who shall therein be committed
        - Pursuant to Law, the Court doth nominate and appoint JOHN NOWLAND
and WILLIAM BAKER as fit and able persons residing in this County to inspect the
package and weigh all Pork, Beef and also the filling of all Tar Pitch and Turpentine
packed or filled for Sale or Exportation and also to inspect and weight all Wheat
Flower made and intended for Exportation within this County for the ensuing year.
The said WILLIAM BAKER in Court took the Oath of his Office
        - Ordered that the Court be adjourned till tomorrow morning eight o'clock
        - The Minutes of these Proceedings were signed
                            " :AENS: CAMPBELL "

p.   - At a Court continued and held for Loudoun County at the Courthouse on
504   Thursday the Tenth day of September one thousand seven hundred and sixty
        one, Before his Majesty's Justices of the Peace for said County, to wit;
            JAMES HAMILTON   NICHOLAS MINOR

AENEAS CAMPBELL   JOSIAS CLAPHAM   and
                GEORGE WEST,   Gent.

- JAMES LEITH, Plt. agt. JAMES INGEO DOZER, Deft.   In Case
By agreement of the parties, this suit is dismissed and it is ordered that Deft. pay
unto Plt. his costs
- ELIZABETH GORAM, an Evidence for JAMES LEITH against JAMES
INGOE DOZER, having attended Court three daies, ordered that JAMES LEITH pay
her seventy five pounds of tobacco for the same
- Messrs. HUNTER, CAMPBELL & COMPANY, Merchts. in Great Britain,
Plts. against JOSHUA HARRISON, otherwise called I JOSHUA HARRISON
of County of Loudoun, Planter, Deft.   In Debt
Discontinued, Plts. not further prosecuting
- JOHN GODDARD, Plt. agt. ROBERT WATSON, Deft.   In Debt
This day came the parties by their Attornies and Deft. prays Oyer of the Writing
which is granted him
- JOHN CAMBDEN, Plt. agt. JEREMIAH COCKRILL, Deft. In Case
This day came the parties by their Attornies and Deft. saving to himself all advan-
tages of Exceptions as well to Plt.'s Writ as to his Declaration prays and has leave to
imparl till next Court and then to plead
- ISAAC NICKOLS, Plt. agt. WILLIAM DODD, otherwise called I WILLLIAM
DODD of Loudoun County, Deft.   In Debt
HUGH WEST comes into Cout and undertakes for Deft. that in case he shall be
cast in this suit that he will pay and satisfy the condemnation of the Court or render
his body to Prison in execution for the same, or that he, the said HUGH, will do it for
him; And Deft. prays Oyer of the Writ, Declaration and Bond and also leave to imparl
till next Court and then to plead which is granted him

p.   Loudoun County Court 10th of September 1761
505   - ANDREW ADAM, Plt. agt. DAVID DAVIS, Deft.   In Case
This day came the parties by their Attornies and Deft. saving to himself all
advantages of Exceptions as well to Plt.'s Writ as to his Declaration, prays and has
leave to imparl till next Courtand then to plead
- RICHARD SPURR, Plt. agt. JAMES COLEMAN, Deft.
In Trespass Assault and Battery
By agreement of the parties this suit is dismissed and it is ordered that Deft. pay
unto Plt. his costs
- THOMAS HARRISON, JAMES NISBET, BENJAMIN GRAYSON and
SPENCE GRAYSON, Exrs. &c. of the Last Will and Testament of BENJA-
MIN GRAYSON, Gent., deced., Plts. agt. GEORGE HARDY, otherwise called
I GEORGE HARDY of Louduun County and Parish of Cameron, Deft. In Debt
WILLIAM HARDY of this County comes into Court and undertakes for Deft. that
in case he shall be cast in this suit he will pay and satisfy the condemnation of the
Court or render his body to Prison in execution for the same, or that he, the said
WILLIAM will do it for him, and Deft. by WILLIAM ELLZEY, his Attorney, saving to
himself all advantages of Exceptions as well to Plt.'s Writ as to his Declaration prays
and has leave to imparl till next Court and then to plead

- ANDREW ADAM, Plt. agt. WILLIAM GOSSETT, JUNR. Deft.   In Case
ROBERT POPKINS and JOHN WALTON, Securities for Deft.'s appearance, by
WILLIAM ELLZEY, their Attorney, saving to themselves all advantages of Excep-
tions as well to Plt.'s Writ as to his Declaration pray and have leave to imparl till next
Court and then to plead
- BENJAMIN GRAYSON, Gent. Plt. agt. WILLIAM FIELDER, Deft. In Case
The Deft. being arrested and not appearing altho' solemnly called, on motion of Plt.
by HUGH WEST, his Attorney, it is ordered that unless Deft. shall appear at next
Court and answer Plt.'s action, Judgment shall then be given the Plt. against him the
Deft. and DANIEL MILLER, who is returned Security for his appearance for his
damages and costs
- WILLIAM GOSSETT, JUNR. Plt. agt. SAMUEL DAVIS, JUNR. Deft.
In Trespass Assault and Battery
The Deft. being returned not found, on motion of Plt.'s Attorney, an Alias Capias is
awarded him returnable here at next Court

p.   Loudoun County Court 10th of September 1761
506   - JOHN TRAMMELL, Plt. against EZEKIEL HICKMAN, Deft.   In Case
This day came the parties by their Attornies and Deft. saving to himself all
advantages of Exceptions as well to Plt.'s Writ as to his Declaration, prays and has
leave to imparl till next Court and then to plead
- BENJAMIN GRAYSON and CRAVEN PEYTON, Plts. against
THOMAS AWBREY, Deft.   In Case
This suit is discontinued, the Plts. not further prosecuting
- WILLIAM DOUGLASS and ELIZABETH his Wife, Admrx. &c. of
STEPHEN LEWIS, Gent., deced., Plts. agt. JOHN DAVIS and MARGARET
his Wife, Admrx. of THOMAS DAVIS, deced., Deft.   In Chancery
On motion of Complts. by their Attorney, time is allowed them till the next Court to
file their Bill
- ROBERT POPKINS, Plt. agt. JOHN PHILLIPS, Deft.   In Case
The Deft. being returned not found, on motion of Plt.'s Attorney an Alias Capias is
awarded him returnable here at next Court
- CHARLES BUTLER, Plt. agt. WILLIAM DOUGLASS, Deft.
In Trespass Assault and Battery and False Imprisonment
Continued till next Cort by consent of parties
- ARTHUR MORTIMORE, Plt. agt. HENRY BREWER, Deft.   In Case
This day came the parties by their Attornies and Deft. saving to himself all advan-
tages of Exception as well to Plt.'s Writ as to his Declaration prays and has leave to
imparl till next Court and then to plead
- BENJAMIN GRAYSON, Gent., Plt. agt. JAMES GOULDING, Deft. In Case
AENEAS CAMPBELL, Gent., in Court undertakes for Deft. that in case he shall
be cast in this suit he shall pay and satisfy the condemnation of the Court or render
his body to Prison in execution for the same, or that he, the said AENEAS, will do it
for him; And Deft. by WILLIAM ELLZEY, his Attorney, saving to himself all advantages of Exceptions as well to Plt.'s Writ

p.   Loudoun County Court 10th of September 1761
507   as to his Declaration prays and has leave to imparl till next Court and then to
         plead
              - FRANCIS PEYTON, Gent., Plt. agt. ANTHONY SEALE, Deft. In Case
This day came the parties by their Attornies and Deft. saving to himself all advantages of Exceptions as well to Plt.'s Writ as to his Declaration, prays and has leave to
imparl till next Court and then to plead
              - JOHN PALMER, Plt. agt. EDWARD SNIKERS, Deft.   In Case
This day came the parties by their Attornies and Deft. saving to himself all advantages of Exceptions as well to Plt.'s Writ as to his Declaration, prays and has leave to
imparl till next Court and then to plead
              - JOHN PALMER, JUNR, Plt. agt. EDWARD SNIKERS, Deft.   In Case
This day came the parties by their Attornies and Deft. saving to himself all advantages of Exceptions as well to Plt.'s Writ as to his Declaration, prays and has leave to
imparl till next Court and then to plead
              - DAVID DAVIS, Plt. agt. JOHN CARLYLE, Deft.   In Case
This day came the parties by their Attornies and Deft. saving to himself all advantages of Exceptions as well to Plt.'s Writ as to his Declaration, prays and has leave to
imparl till next Court and then to plead
              - HECTOR ROSS, Plt. agt. JOHN CALLIHAN & THOMAS KELLY, Defts.
         In Debt
The Defts. being returned not found, on motion of Plt.'s Attorney an Alias Capias is
awarded him returnable here at next Court
              - JOHN STONE, Plt. agt. JOHN PALMER, DANIEL PALMER and THO-
              MAS PALMER, Defts.   In Trespass
The Defts. being returned not found, on motion of Plt.'s Attorney an Alias Capias is
awarded him returnable here at next Court
              - ISAAC FOSTER, Plt. agt. BENJAMIN HUTCHISON, Deft. In Case
This suit is discontinued, the Plt. not further prosecuting

p.   Loudoun County Court 10th of September 1761
508   - THOMAS SELF, Plt. agt. ARTHUR MORTIMORE, Deft.
         In Trespass Assault and Battery
This day came the parties by their Attornies and Deft. saving to himself all advantages of Exceptions as well to Plt.'s Writ as to his Declaration, prays and has leave to
imparl till next Court and then to plead
              - THOMAS SELF, Plt. agt. ARTHUR MORTIMORE, Deft.   In Case
This day came the parties by their Attornies and Deft. saving to himself all advantages of Exceptions as well to Plt.'s Writ as to his Declaration, prays and has leave to
imparl till next Court and then to plead
              - HENRY BREWER, Plt. agt. ARTHUR MORTIMORE, Deft. In Case
This day came the parties by their Attornies and Deft. saving to himself all advantages of Exceptions as well to Plt.'s Writ as to his Declaration, prays and has leave to
imparl till next Court and then to plead
              - JOHN PALMER, Plt. agt. EDWARD SNIGGERS, Deft.   In Case
This day came the parties by their Attornies and Deft. saving to himself all advantages of Exception as well to Plt.'s Writ as to his Declaration, prays and has leave to

imparl till next Court and then to plead

      - THOMAS PALMER, Plt. agt. EDWARD SNIGGERS, Deft.   In Case

This suit is discontinued, Plt. not further prosecuting

      - WILLIAM HARBIN, Plt. agt. MARY ANSLEY, Admrx. of the Last Will &
      Testament of HENRY ANSLEY, deced., Deft.   In Debt

This day came the parties by their Attornies and Deft. prays Oyer of the Bond, &c.
which is granted him

      - NICHOLAS MINOR and JAMES LANE, Gent., Churchwardens for the time
      being for the Parish of Cameron in the County of Loudoun who sue in behalf of
      themselves and the pooor of the said Parish and their use; Plts. against
      CATHARINE STEWART, Spinster, Deft.   In Debt

This suit is dismissed, (the Fine being paid) and it is ordered that Deft. pay unto

p.   Loudoun County Court 10th of September 1761
509   Plts. their costs

      - ABRAHAM DAWSON, Plt. agt. JOSEPH CALDWELL, Deft.
      In Trespass Assault and Battery

The Plt. not further prosecuting, on motion of Deft. by HUGH WEST, his Attorney,
it is ordered that this suit be dismissed and that Plt. pay unto Deft. his costs

      - ROBERT PEYTON, an Infant under the age of twenty one years by JOHN
      PEYTON, his Guardian, Plt. agt. JAMES LEITH, Deft.   In Case

This day came the parties by their Attornies and Deft. saving to himself all advantages of Exceptions as well to Plt.'s Writ as to his Declaration, prays and has leave to
imparl till next Court and then to plead

      - THOMSON MASON, Plt. agt. ROBERT SANDFORD, JUNR., Deft.
      Upon a Writ of Scire Facias

This day came Plt. by HUGH WEST, his Attorney, and Deft. altho' solemnly called
came not; Therefore it is considered by the Court that Plt. ought to have execution
against Deft. for the sum of five pounds, sixty four pounds of nett tobacco and seven
shillings and six pence and his costs by him in this behalf expended, and Deft. in
mercy &c.

      - THOMSON MASON, Plt. agt. FRANKLIN PERRY, Deft.
      Upon a Writ of Scire Facias

The Sherif having returned that Deft. is not to be found in his Bailiwick, ordered
that an Alias Scire Facias be issued against him returnable here at next Court

      - WILLIAM SAUNDERS, Plt. agt. THOMAS AWBREY, Admr. of all and
      singular the goods & chattels rights and credits of WALTER ENGLISH, deced.
      Deft.   In Chancery

The Deft. being returned not to be found, on motion of Plt.'s Attorney a new Summons is awarded him returnable here at next Court

      - HENRY BOGGESS, JUNR., Plt. against SAMPSON TURLEY, Deft.
      In Trespass Assault and Battery

This day came the parties by their Attornies and Deft. saving to himself all advantages of Exceptions as well to Plt.'s Writ as to his Declaration, prays and has leave to
imparl till next Court and then to plead

      - Ordered that CHRISTIAN HARNE be added to the List of Tithables taken
for this County this present year

p.   Loudoun County Court 10th of September 1761
510   - SAMPSON TURLEY, Plt. agt. HENRY BOGGESS, JUNR., Deft. In Debt
        This day came the parties by their Attornies and Deft. saving to himself all
advantages of Exceptions as well to Plt.'s Writ as to his Declaration, prays and has
leave to imparl till next Court and then to plead
        - WILLIAM ELLZEY, Plt. agt. JOHN ANDERSON, Deft.   In Case
The Defendant being returned not to be found, on motion of Plt.'s Attorney, an Alias
Capias is awarded him returnable here at next Court
        - JOSEPH JONES, Plt. agt. JOHN BOND, Deft.   In Case
This day came the parties by their Attornies and Deft. saving to himself all advantages of Exceptions as well to Plt.'s Writ as to his Declaration, prays and has leave to
imparl till next Court and then to plead
        - THOMAS HARRISON, JAMES NISBET, BENJAMIN GRAYSON and
        SPENCE GRAYSON, Exrs. of the Last Will and Testament of BENJAMIN
        GRAYSON, Gent., deced., Plts. against JOHN KING, Deft.   In Case
The Sherif having returned no effects in the former Attachment, on motion of Plts.
by their Attorney, it is ordered that another Attachment issue against Deft.'s Estate
for four thousand pounds of crop tobacco and fifty shillings current money and costs
returnable here at next Court
        - FRANCIS PEYTON and NICHOLAS MINOR, Gent., Churchwardens for the
        time being for the Parish of Cameron in the County of Loudoun, Plts. against
        ANN GRIFFIN, Deft.   In Debt
The Deft. being again returned not to be found, on motion of Plts. by their Attorney
another Plurius Capias is awarded them returnable here at the next Court
        - RICHARD SNOWDEN, Plt. against BENJAMIN MUSGROVE otherwise
        called I BENJAMIN MUSGROVE of ANN ARUNDELL County, Deft. In Debt
ANDREW ADAM of this County comes into Court and undertakes for Deft. that in
case he shall be cast in this suit, he shall pay and satisfy the condemnation of the
Court or render his body to Prison in execution for the same or that he, the said
ANDREW, will do it for him; And Deft. by FRANCIS DADE, his Attorney prays Oyer
of the Bond, &c., which is granted him

p.   Loudoun County Court 10th of September 1761
511   - RICHARD SNOWDEN, Plt. agt. BENJAMIN MUSGROVE, Deft In Case
        ANDREW ADAM of this County comes into Court and undertakes for Deft.
that in case he shall be cast in this suit that he shall pay and satisfy the condemnation of the Court or render his body to Prison in execution for the same or that he, the
said ANDREW, will do it for him; And Deft. saving to himself all advantages of Exceptions as well to Plt.'s Writ as to his Declaration, prays and has leave to imparl till
next Court and then to plead
        - REBECCA EADES, an Infant under the age of twenty one years by THO-
        MAS HAMILTON her Guardian and next Friend, Plt. against JOHN
        LACKEY and JACOB GARDNER, Defts.   In Trespass Assault and Battery
The Deft., JACOB GARDNER, being again returned not found, on Plt.'s motion
anothr Plurius Capias is awarded her returnable here at next Court
        - CRAVEN PEYTON, Assignee of ARTHUR CHARLTON, Plt. agt.
        JOSEPH CLAYPOOLE, otherwise called JOSEPH CLAYPOOLE of FAIRFAX

County in the Colony of Virginia, Farmer, Deft.   In Debt

The Attachment awarded against Deft.'s Estate being returned executed on one narrow Ax, and Deft. not appearing to replevy the same, it is considered by the Court that Plt. recover against Deft. five pounds, nineteen shillings and three pence current money of Virginia and his costs by him in this behalf expended, and Defendant in mercy, &c., And it is ordered that the Sherif make sale of the attached Ax according to Law and render the money arising from the sale to Plt. towards satisfying of his Debt and costs aforesaid and that he return an Account of the sale to the Court

        - ANDREW ADAM, Plt. agt. THOMAS PHILLIPS, Deft.   In Debt

The Deft. being returned not to be found, on motion of Plt.'s Attorney an Alias Capias is awarded him returnable here at next Court

        - JOSIAS CLAPHAM, Gent., Plt. agt. THOMAS JONES, Deft. In Trespass

This suit is discontinued, Plt. not further prosecuting

        - BENJAMIN GRAYSON and STACEY his Wife, Admrx. of BURGESS
        BERKLEY, deced., Complts. agt. WILLIAM BERKLEY, Deft.   In Chancery

The Deft. still failing to answer Complts.'s Bill, it is ordered that an Attachment be issued against him returnable here at next Court

p.   Loudoun County Court 10th of September 1761

512   - JOHN GORAM, a witness for JAMES LEITH against JAMES INGOE

        DOZER having attended Court three daies, ordered that JAMES LEITH pay him seventy five pounds of tobacco for the same

        - JAMES HOOK, Plt. against WILLIAM COLVIN, Deft. Upon an Attachment

This day came Plt. by WILLIAM ELLZEY, his Attorney, and Deft. came not altho' solemnly called. Therefore it is considered by the Court that Plt. recover against Deft. one thousand five hundred thirty three pounds of tobacco and eight pounds, nine shillings and three pence and his costs by him in this behalf expended and Deft. in mercy, &c. The Sherif having returned that he had levied the Attachment on two hogsheads of tobacco and two Horses and a Mare and Colt (which are ordered to be sold to satisfy a Judgment obtained by JOSIAS CLAPHAM, Gent., against the Deft.), it is ordered that the Sherif pay the overplus arising from the sale of the goods, after CLAPHAM's Judgment is satisfied, to Plt. towards satisfying of his Debt and costs aforesaid

        - JOHN TRAMMELL, Plt. agt. WILLIAM COLVIN Deft.

        Upon an Attachment

JOSIAS CLAPHAM, Gent., Garnishee being sworn declares he has nothing and thereupon he is discharged. CHARLES STAFFORD and THMAS PYBURN being also summoned as Garnishees in this suit, and failing to appear, it is ordered that an Attachment issue against them for their contempt returnable here at next Court and the Attachment is continued till next Court to be further served

        - JAMES HOPKINS, Assignee of JOHN CARLYLE and JOHN PAGAN, Plt.
        agt. JOSIAS CLAPHAM, otherwise called I JOSIAS CLAPHAM of FAIRFAX
        County, Mercht., Deft.   In Debt

This day came the parties by their Attornies and thereupon came also a Jury to wit;

JOHN HERYFORD	JOSHUA GORE	MARTIN ARMSTRONG
WILLIAM BAKER	EZEKIEL HICKMAN	JESSE LUM
THOMAS SORRELL	JOHN TRAMMELL	CHARLES CHILTON
THOMAS LEWIS	JONATHAN DAVIS and	WILLIAM DODD

who being elected tried and sworn the truth to speak upon the issue joined, upon their Oath do say that Deft. hath not paid to Plt. thirty eight pounds, eight shillings and ten pence currency, the Debt in the Declaration mentioned, in manner and form as Plt. against him hath complained and they do assess Plt.'s damages by occasion of the Detention of the Debt to one penny besides his costs. Therefore it is considered by the Court that Plt. recover against Deft. the thirty eight pounds, eight shillings and ten pence currency with legal Interest thereon from the 27th day of September 1753 till paid, together with his damages aforesaid in form aforesaid assessed and his costs about his suit in this behalf expended, and Deft. in mercy, &c.

p.   Loudoun County Court 10th of September 1761
513   - CRAVEN PEYTON and CHARLES WEST, having taken the Oath to his
        Majesty's Person and Government and subscribed the Abjuration Oath and
Test were on motion of WILLIAM WEST, Gent., sworn and admitted his Under Sheriffs and then said CRAVEN and CHARLES took the Oath appointed by the Tobacco Law
        - SARAH LEWIS, Widow and Relict of THOMAS LEWIS, deced., Complts.
        agt.   WILLIAM DOUGLASS and ELIZABETH his Wife, late ELIZABETH
        LEWIS, Defts.   In Chancery
The Defts. failing to answer Complts.'s Bill, it is ordered that an Attachment issue against them returnable here at next Court
        - BENJAMIN GRAYSON, Gent., Plt. agt. JOHN DAVIS, Deft.   In Case
The Plt. not further prosecuting, on motion of Deft. by WILLIAM ELLZEY, his Attorney, it is ordered that this suit be dismissed and that Plt. pay unto Deft. his costs
        - FRANCIS JOHN, Plt. against JOHN KING   On Petition
The Plt. not further prosecuting, on motion of Deft. by BENJAMIN SEBASTIAN, his Attorney it is ordered that the Petition be dismissed and that Plt. pay unto Deft. his costs
        - EDWARD TRAFFORD, Esqr., Plt. agt. GEORGE HARDY, JUNR., and
        WILLIAM HARDY, SENR., Defts.   In Debt
The Defts. plead paiment and for Trial thereof put themselves upon the Country and Plt. likewise. Therefore it is commanded the Sherif that he cause to come here at next Court twelve good and lawful men by whom, &c.
        - SIMON PEARSON and MILKEY PEARSON his Wife, WILLIAM STARKE
        and SUSANNA STARKE his Wife, EZEKIEL HICKMAN and ELIZABETH
        HICKMAN his Wife and WILLIAM TRAMMELL, Plts. agt.
        JOHN TRAMMELL and SAMPSON TRAMMELL, Defts. In Chancery
The Defts. failing to answer the Bill of Complts., it is ordered that an Attachment issue against them returnable here at next Court
        - JOHN GLADIN, Plt. agt. JOSEPH CLAYPOLE, Deft.   In Case
By consent of the parties, the Order of Arbitration in this Cause is discontinued and thereupon Deft. pleads Not Guilty and for Trial putteth himself upon the Country, and Plt. likewise, Therefore it is commanded the Sherif that he cause to come here at next Court twelve good and lawful men by whom, &c.

p.   <u>Loudoun County Court 10th of September 1761</u>
514   - WILLIAM MEAD, Plt. agt. JOHN DAVIS and MARGARET his Wife,
      Admrx. of all and singular the goods and chattels of THOMAS DAVIS, deced.,
      Defts.   In Debt
Continued till next Court by consent of the parties
     - JAMES McCARTY, Plt. agt. SAMPSON TRAMMELL, Deft.   In Case
The Deft. saith that he is Not Guilty and for Trial thereof putteth himself upon the
Country, and Plt. likewise, Therefore it is commanded the Sherif that he cause to
come here at next Court twelve good and lawful men by whom, &c.
     - BENJAMIN SHACKLIFF, Infant under the age of twenty one years by
      BENJAMIN SHACKLIFF, his Father and next Friend, Plt. agt.
      SHARDRICK LEWELLEN, Deft.   In Trespass Assault and Battery
The Deft. saith he is Not Guilty and for Trial thereof putteth himself upon the
Country, and Plt. likewise, Therefore it is commanded the Sherif that he cause to
come here at next Court twelve good and lawful men by whom, &c.
     - CHARLES COLE, Plt. against HUGH FOUCH, Deft.
     In Trespass Assault and Battery
The Deft. saith he is Not Guilty and for Trial thereof putteth himself upon the
Country, and Plt. likewise; Therefore it is commanded the Sherif that he cause to
come here at next Court twelve good and lawful men by whom, &c.
     - JOHN RILEY, Plt. against EZEKIEL HICKMAN, Deft.
     In Trespass Assault and Battery
Continued till next Court by consent of the parties
     - JOHN ELLIOT, Plt. agt. THOMAS SELF, Deft.   In Case
Continued till next Court by consent of the parties
     - SARAH HICKS, Exrx. of the Last Will and Testament of WILLIAM HICKS,
      Esqr., deced., Plt. against JOB JENKINS and JOHN MORRIS, Defts. In Debt
Continued till next Court
     - MARY JORDAN, Plt. agt. LEROY HUGHLET, Deft..   In Case
The Deft. saith he is Not Guilty and for Trial thereof putteth himself upon the

p.   <u>Loudoun County Court 10th of September 1761</u>
515   County and Plt. likewise, Therefore it is commanded that the Sherif cause to
      come here at the next Court twelve good and lawful men by whom, &c.
     - JAMES INGOE DOZER, Plt. agt. JAMES McKENNEY, Deft. In Debt
The Deft. pleads paiment and for Trial thereof putteth himself upon the Country
and Plt. likewise, Therefore it is commanded that the Sherif cause to come here at
next Court twelve good and lawful men by whom, &c.
     - BENJAMIN GRAYSON, Mercht., Plt. agt. WILLIAM ..HARDY, Deft.
     In Case
The Defendant saith he did not assume upon himself in manner and form as Plt.
against him hath declared and for Trial thereof putteth himself upon the Country
and Plt. likewise, Therefore it is commaned that the Sherif cause to come here at next
Court twelve good and lawful men by whom, &c.
     - JOHN HERYFORD, Plt. agt. JOSEPH STEPHENS, Deft.
     In Trespass Assault and Battery
The Deft. saith he is Not Guilty and for Trial thereof putteth himself upon the

Country, and Plt. likewise, Therefore it is commanded that the Sherif cause to come here at next Court twelve good and lawful men by whom, &c.

- JOHN MOSS, JUNR., Plt. agt. HENRY ANSLEY, Deft.   In Case

This suit abates by the death of Deft.

- EZEKIEL HICKMAN, Plt. agt. THOMAS AWBREY, Deft.

Upon a Writ of Scire Facias

The Deft. pleads paiment and for Trial putteth himself upon the Country and Plt. likewise; Therefore it is commanded that the Sherif cause to come here at next Court twelve good and lawful men by whom, &c.

- JOHN GODDARD, Plt. agt. SAMPSON TURLEY, Deft.

In Trespass Assault and Battery

The Deft. saith he is Not Guilty and for Trial thereof putteth himself upon the Country, and Plt. likewise, Therefore it is commanded that the Sherif cause to come here at next Court twelve good and lawful men by whom, &c.

p.   Loudoun County Court 10th of September 1761
516   - JOHN GODDARD, Plt. agt. HENRY WISHEART, Deft.

In Trespass Assault and Battery

The Deft. saith he is Not Guilty and for Trial putteth himself upon the Country and Plt. likewise, Therefore it is commanded that the Sherif cause to come here at next Court twelve good and lawful men by whom, &c.

- Messrs. JAMES HUNTER and COMPANY, Plts. agt. MARGARET JENKINS, Admrx. of all and singular the goods and chattels rights and credits of SAMUEL JENKINS, deced., Deft.   In Case

Continued till next Court

- Messrs. PATRICK and WILLIAM BOGLE and COMPANY, Plts. agt. WILLIAM OWSLEY, otherwise called I WILLIAM OWSLEY of FAIRFAX County, Deft.   In Debt

Continued till next Court by consent of the parties

- Messrs. PATRICK and WILLIAM BOGLE and COMPANY, Plts. agt. JOHN GORAM otherwise called I JOHN GORAM of FAIRFAX County, Deft.   In Debt

Continued till next Court by consent of the parties

- Messrs. PATRICK and WILLIAM BOGLE and COMPANY, Plts. agt. JOHN CHAMP, Deft.   In Case

Continued till next Court by consent of the parties

- SIMON PEARSON and MILKEY PEARSON, his Wife, Complts. agt. JOHN TRAMMELL and SAMPSON TRAMMELL, Exrs. of the Last Will and Testament of JOHN TRAMMELL, deced., Defts.   In Chancery

The Defts. failing to answer the Bill of Complts., it is ordered that an Attachment issue against them returnable here at next Court

- FRANCIS PEYTON, Gent., Plt. agt. THOMAS DONOHOE, Deft. In Case

Continued till next Court by consent of the parties

- WILLIAM DODD, Plt. agt. JOHN RICHARDS, Deft. In Debt

The Deft. saith he did not assume upon himself in manner and form as Plt. against him hath declared and of this he putteth himself upon the County, and the

Plt. likewise, Therefore it is commanded that the Sherif cause to come here at next Court twelve good and lawful men by whom, &c.

    - GEORGE SANGSTER, Plt. against HUGH BLACK, Deft.   In Debt
Continued till next Court by consent of the parties

    - Absent. NICHOLAS MINOR, Gent.

    - An Indenture of Feofment between NICHOLAS MINOR of one part and BENJAMIN EDWARDS of other part and the Memorandum of Livery of Seisen thereon endorsed were acknowledged by said NICHOLAS and ordered to be recorded

    - LEVI WILKS, Plt. agt. EDWARD THOMPSON, Deft. In Covenant
This suit is dismissed, being agreed by the parties

    - Ordered that the Sherif of this County summon JAMES COLEMAN and JANE his Wife to appear here at next Court to answer an Information exhibited against them for incestuous copulation

    - JACOB LASSWELL on his Petition is by the Court discharged from the paiment of Levies & Poll Tax for the future

    - Ordered that DAVID DAVIS and his Tithable, to wit, Negroe Sampson, be added to the List of Tithables taken for this County this present year

    - Ordered that JOHN YOUNT and his Tithable, to wit, MICHAEL BURGEN, be added to the List of Tithables for this County this present year

    - Ordered that the Sherif summon twenty four of the most capable Freeholders of this County to appear here on the second Tuesday in November next to serve as a Grand Jury of Inquest for the body of this County

    - Present. NICHOLAS MINOR, Gent.

    - CORNELIUS DONOHOE and MARGARET his Wife, JOHN SINKLER and SARAH his Wife and ISAAC FOUCH and MARY his Wife, Complts. against JANE McDOWELL and ANN McDOWELL, Exrs. of MARY JENNINGS, deced., Defts.   In Chancery
On motion of Defts. by their Attorney, further time is allowed them till next Court to answer the Bill of Complainants

    - FERDINANDO O'NEAL, Plt. agt. JOHN KILLIHAM, Deft. In Case
Continued till next Court by consent of the parties

    - Messrs. JOHN CHAMPE and COMPANY, Plts. agt. JESPER GRANT otherwise called I JESPER GRANT of PRINCE WILLIAM County, Deft. In Debt
The Plt. not further prosecuting, on motion of Deft. by BENJAMIN SEBASTIAN

p.   <u>Loudoun County Court 10th of September 1761</u>
518   his Attorney, it is ordered that this suit be dismissed and that Plt. pay unto Deft. his costs

    - JOHN JOHNSON who as well for us as for himself in this behalf prosecutes Plt. agt. ROBERT WOOD, Deft.   In Debt
Continued till next Court by consent of the parties

    - WILLIAM DOUGLASS and ELIZABETH DOUGLASS his Wife, Plts. agt. EZEKIEL HICKMAN, Deft.   In Case
The Deft. saith he is Not Guilty and for Trial thereof putteth himself upon the Country and Plts. likewise, Therefore it is commanded that the Sherif cause to come here at next Court twelve good and lawful men by whom, &c.

- JOHN WILLIS, Plt. agt. JOSEPH WEST, Deft.   In Case
On motion of Deft., it is ordered that unless Plt. shall find Security for costs at the next Court, this suit be then dismissed with costs
     - MOSES BOTTS, Plt. agt. CHARLES CHINN and ELIJAH CHINN, Defts.
     In Debt
Continued till next Court by consent of the parties
     - THOMAS DONOHUE, Plt. agt. SAMUEL WINN, Deft.   In Trespass
Continued till next Court by consent of the parties
     - MICHAEL VAN BUSCART, Plt. agt. JOSIAS CLAPHAM, Gent., Deft.
     In Case
The Deft. saith that he did not assume upon himself in manner and form as Plt. against him hath declared and of this he putteth himself upon the Country, and Plt. likewise, Therefore it is commanded that the Sherif cause to come here at next Court twelve good and lawful men by whom, &c.
     - The Petition of SAMUEL WINN against THOMAS LEWIS is continued till next Court at motion and costs of Plt.
     - CHARLES CHILTON, an Evidence for THOMAS LEWIS at the suit of SAMUEL WINN, having attended Court three daies, ordered that said SAMUEL pay him seventy five pounds of tobacco for the same, the Cause being continued at his costs
     - JACOB GARDNER, an Evidence of THOMAS LEWIS at the suit of SAMUEL WINN, having attended Court three daies, ordered that said SAMUEL pay him seventy five pounds of

p.   Loudoun County Court 10th of September 1761
519   tobacco for the same, the Cause being continued at his costs
     - THOMAS RODEN an Evidence for THOMAS LEWIS at the suit of SAMUEL WINN, having attended three daies and for travelling sixty miles from FREDERICK County and returning once, ordered that said SAMUEL pay him two hundred fifty five pounds of tobacco for the same, the Cause being continued at his costs
     - FRANKLIN PERRY, Plt. agt. ABRAHAM BARNES, Deft.   In Case
Continued till next Court by consent of the parties
     - THOMAS FIELDS, Gent., Plt. agt. WILLIAM OWSLEY, Deft.
     In Trespass Asssault and Battry and False Imprisonment
Continued till next Court by consent of the parties
     - RICHARD SNOWDEN, Plt. agt. ZACHARIAH WARD, otherwise called ZACHARIAH WARD of FREDERICK County, Carpenter, Deft.   In Debt
This suit abates by the death of the Deft.
     - JOSHUA HICKMAN, Complt. agt. EZEKIEL HICKMAN, Deft.
     In Chancery
On motion of Complt. by his Attorney, further time is allowed till next Court to file his Bill
     - MAURICE TURNER, Plt. agt. JOSEPH JONES, Deft.   In Case
HUGH WEST, Gent., comes into Court and undertakes for Deft. that in case he shall be cast in this suit he shall pay and satisfy the condemnation of the Court or render his body to Prison in execution for the same or that he, the said MAURICE,

will do it for him; And Deft. prays and has further leave to imparl till next Court and
then to plead
>   - THOMAS HARRISON, JAMES NISBET, BENJAMIN GRAYSON and
>   SPENCE GRAYSON, Exrs. of the Last Will and Testament of BENJAMIN
>   GRAYSON, Gent., deced., Plts. against SAMPSON TURLEY, Deft. In Case

By consent of the parties, the Order for Arbitration in this Cause is discontinued
and thereupon Deft. saith he did not assume upon himself in manner and form as
Plts. against him hath declared and of this he putteth himself upon the Country, and
Plts. likewise, Therefore it is commanded that the Sherif cause to come here at next
Court twelve good and lawful men, &c.

p.   Loudoun County Court 10th of September 1761
520   - JOHN HOUGH, Exr. of the Last Will and Testament of JOHN POULT-
>   NEY, deced., Plt. agt. WILLIAM COLVIN, Deft.   In Case

The Defendant pleads paiment and for Trial thereof putteth himself upon the Country and Plt. likewise, Therefore it is considered that the Sherif cause to come here at
next Court twelve good and lawful men by whom, &c.
>   - THOMAS SLIGH, Mercht., Plt. agt. RALPH BROADIK otherwise lately
>   called, I RALPH BROADAX, of BALTIMORE County, Planter, Deft. In Debt

The Deft. pleads paiment and for Trial thereof putteth himself upon the Country
and Plt. likewise; Therefore it is commanded that the Sherif cause to come her at
next Court twelve good and lawful men by whom, &c.
>   - JOSHUA HICKMAN, Plt. agt. EZEKIAL HICKMAN, Deft. In Detinue

The Deft. saith he does not detain the slave in the Declaration mentioned in manner and form as Plt. against him hath declared and of this he putteth himself upon the
Country and Plt. likewise, Therefore it is commanded that the Sherif cause to come
here at next Court twelve good and lawful men by whom, &c.
>   - FARLAN BALL, Plt. agt. JOHN BISHOP, Deft.   In Debt

Continued till next Court by consent of the parties
>   - LEWIS ELLZEY, Gent., Plt. agt. JOHN BISHOP, Deft.   In Case

This day came the parties by their Attornies and Deft. saving to himself all advantages of Exceptions as well to Plt.'s Writ as to his Declaration, prays and has leave to
imparl till next Court and then to plead
>   - BENJAMIN GRAYSON, Gent., Plt. agt. SAMPSON TURLEY, Deft. In Case

By consent of the parties, the Order for Arbitration in this Cause is discontinued
and thereupon Deft. saith that he did not assume upon himself in manner and form as
Plt. against him hath complained and of this he putteth himself upon the Country,
and Plt. likewise, Therefore it is commanded that the Sherif cause to come here at
next Court twelve good and lawful men by whom, &c.

p.   Loudoun County Court 10th of September 1761
521   - THOMAS BOTTS, Plt. agt. CHARLES CHINN alias CHARLES
>   DOLEMAN, Deft. In Case

This day came the parties by their Attornies and Deft. prays and has further leave
to imparl till next Court and then to plead
>   - JOHN HOUGH, Plt. agt. THOMAS PHILLIPS otherwise called I THOMAS
>   PHILLIPS of County of Loudoun and Colony of Virginia, Deft.   In Debt

The Deft. not appearing tho' again solemnly called, on motion of Plt.'s Attorney it is considered that Plt. recover against Deft. and JENKINS PHILLIPS, the Security for his appearance, three pounds, thirteen shillings and seven pence current money of Virginia, the Debt in the Declaration mentioned, with lawfull Interest thereon from the first day of August 1759 till paid and his costs by him in this behalf expended, and the Deft. in mercy, &c.

- WILLIAM HATCHER, Plt. agt. THOMAS PHILLIPS, Deft.   In Debt

The Deft. not appearing tho' again solemnly called, on motion of Plt. by his Attorney, it is considered that Plt. recover against Deft. and JENKINS PHILLIPS, the Security for his appearance, eight pounds, ten shillings current money of Virginia, the Debt in the Declaration mentioned, with lawful Interest thereon from the nineteenth day of August 1760 till paid, and his costs by him in this behalf expended, and the Deft. in mercy, &c.

- NICHOLAS MINOR and FRANCIS PEYTON, Gent., Churchwardens for the time being for the Parish of Cameron in the County of Loudoun who sue for the use of the said Parish, Plts. against MARY MARTIN, Deft.   In Debt

The Deft. filed a Demurrer which Plts. join and the Cause is continued till next Court

- NICHOLAS MINOR and FRANCIS PEYTON, Gent., Churchwardens for the time being for the Parish of Cameron in the County of Loudoun who sue for the use of the said Parish, Plts. against MARY WINSOR, Deft.   In Debt

The Deft. not appearing tho' again solemnly called. On motion of Plts. by their Attorney, it is considered that Plts. recover against Deft. fifty shillings or five hundred pounds of tobacco and cask, eighty two pounds of nett tobacco and fifteen shillings or one hundred and fifty pounds of tobacco, the Debt in the Declaration mentioned, and their costs by them in this behalf expended, and the Deft. in mercy, &c.

- Ordered that the Surveyor of the Road between the SUGAR LAND RUN and BROAD RUN and the Surveyor between BROAD RUN and GOOSE CREEK clear a Road over BROAD RUN just below the Bridge

p.   Loudoun County Court 10th of September 1761
522   - NICHOLAS MINOR and FRANCIS PEYTON, Gent., Churchwardens for the time being for the Parish of Cameron in the County of Loudoun who sue for the use of the Parish, Plts. agt. ELIZABETH GRANTHAM, Deft. In Debt

The Deft. filed a Demurrer which Plts. join and the Cause is continued till next Court

- THOMAS HAMILTON, Plt. agt. JOHN FOUCH, Deft.
In Trespass Assaault and Battery

Continued till next Court by consent of the parties

- THOMAS HAMILTON, Plt. agt. HUGH FOUCH, Deft.
In Trespass Assault and Battery

Continued till next Court by consent of the parties

- DENNIS DALLIS, Plt. agt. JOHN PYLES, Deft.
In Trespass Assault and Battery

By agreement of the parties this suit is dismissed, and it is ordered that Deft. pay unto Plt. his costs

- EDWARD HARDIN, Plt. agt. JOSIAS CLAPHAM, Gent., Deft. In Debt
The Deft. pleads paiment and for Trial thereof putteth himself upon the Country
and Plt. likewise; Therefore it is commanded that the Sherif cause to come here at
next Court twelve good and lawful men by whom, &c.

- THOMAS HARRISON, JAMES NISBET, BENJAMIN GRAYSON and
SPENCE GRAYSON, Exrs. of the Last Will and Testament of BENJAMIN
GRAYSON, Gent., deced., Plts. agt. CHARLES MORRIS, otherwise called I
CHARLES MORRIS of PRINCE WILLIAM County, Planter, Deft. In Debt
The Deft. not appearing tho' again solemnly called, on motion of Plts. by their
Attorney, it is consdiered that Plts. recover against Deft. and WILLIAM WEST,
Gent. the Security for his appearance, six pounds, twelve shillings and two pence cur-
rent money of Virginia, the Debt in the Declaration mentioned, and their costs by
them in this behalf expended, and the Deft. in mercy, &c., But this Judgment is to be
discharged by paiment of three pounds, six shillings and one penny farthing current
money of Virginia with lawful Interest thereon from the twentieth day of October
1754 till paid and the costs

- Ordered that HUGH WEST, Gent., put in suit a Bond from JOHN TRAM-
MELL to the Justices of this Court for keeping in repair the Bridge over BROAD
RUN

p.   Loudoun County Court 10th of September 1761
523   - JOHN MINOR and ELIZABETH his Wife, late ELIZABETH ELLZEY,
      under the age of twenty one years, by NICHOLAS MINOR their next Friend,
      Plts. against JOHN TRAMMELL otherwise called I JOHN TRAMMELL of
      Loudoun County and Colony of Virginia, Planter, Deft.   In Debt
The Deft. pleads paiment and for Trial thereof putteth himself upon the Country
and Plts. likewise; Therefore it is commanded that the Sherif cause to come at next
Court twelve good and lawful men by whom, &c.

- BENJAMIN GRAYSON, Gent., Plt. agt. JACOB MORRIS, Deft. In Case
The Deft. saith he did not assume upon himself in manner and form as Plt. against
him hath declared and of this he putteth himself upon the Country, and Plt. likewise,
Therefore it is commanded that the Sherif cause to come at next Court twelve good
and lawful men by whom, &c.

- JAMES COMPTON, Plt. agt. JAMES HOOK, Deft.   In Trespass
This day came the parties by their Attornies and Deft. prays and has further leave
to imparl till next Court and then to plead

- HENRY CLAY, Plt. agt. PATRICK COLVERT, Deft.
In Trespass Assault and Battery
The Deft. not appearing tho' again solemnly called, Therefore on motion of Plt.'s
Attorney, it is ordered that the Order of last Court be confirmed and that the
damages be ascertained by a Jury at the next Court

- JOSEPH POLLARD who as well for us as for himself in this behalf prose-
cutes, Plt. against ROBERT SANDFORD, Deft. In Debt
Continued till next Court by consent of the parties

- WILLIAM DODD, Plt. against MICHAEL VAN BUSKARCK, Deft. In Debt
JOHN ST. CLAIR and WILLIAM WOLLARD, Securities for Deft.'s appearance,
plead paiment and for the Trial thereof put themselves upon the Country, and Plt.

likewise, Therefore it is commanded that the Sherif cause to come here at next Court twelve good and lawful men by whom, &c.

- Ordered that JOHN HERYFORD and his Tithables, to wit, Negroes Joseph, Moll and Margaret be added to the List of Tithables taken for this County this present year

p. Loudoun County Court 10th of September 1761
524 - WILLIAM ELLZEY, Assignee of JAMES INGOE DOZER, Plt. against JOHN DAVIS, Deft.   In Debt

The Deft. pleads paiment and for Trial thereof putteth himself upon the Country and Plt. likewise, Therefore it is commanded that the Sherif cause to come her at next Court twelve good and lawful men by whom, &c.

- JOSEPH WEST, Plt. agt. FRANCIS BALLENGER, Deft.
In Trespass Assault and Battery
Discontinued, the Plt. not further prosecuting

- WILLIAM ELLZEY, Guardain of SPENCE GRAYSON, is excused from rendering any Account of the Profits of the Estate of the said Orphan for the future and it is ordered that Process issue against the other Guardians of Orphans who ought to have rendered their Accounts to this Court and have failed therein returnable here at next Court to compel them to render such Accounts at that time

- DAVID ROSS, Plt. agt. JOHN ROSS DEWITT otherwise called I JOHN ROSS DEWITT of FAIRFAX County, Deft.   In Debt

WILLIAM ROSS of this County comes into Court and undertakes for Deft. that in case he shall be cast in this suit that he will pay and satisfy the condemantion of the Court or render his body to Prison in execution for the same, or that he, the said WILLLAM, will do it for him; And Deft. in his proper person prays Oyer of the Writing Obligatory which is granted him

- WILLIAM OWSLEY, Plt. agt. JAMES RODGERS, Deft.   In Debt

JAMES LEITH, CHARLES LEWIS, WILLIAM HARDY, BENJAMIN CHANDLER and JACOB GARDNER of this County come into Court and undertake for the Deft. that in case he shall be cast in this suit he shall pay and satisfy the condemnation of the Court or render his body to Prison in execution for the same, or that they the said JAMES LEITH, CHARLES LEWIS, WILLIAM HARDY, BENJAMIN CHANDLER and JACOB GARDNER will do it for him; And Deft. by BENJAMIN SEBASTIAN, his Attorney, prays Oyer of the Writing Obligatory and also leave to imparl till next Court and then to plead which is granted him

- BENJAMIN EDWARDS, Plt. agt. JAMES LAYTON, Admr. &c. of WILLIAM LAYTON, deced., Deft.   In Covenant

The Deft. saith that the Intestate in his life time did truly perform and keep all and singular the Covenants and Agreements on his part to be performed charged by Plt. in his Declaration against him and prays the same may be inquired of by the Country and Plt. doth likewise the same

p. Loudoun County Court 10th of September 1761
525 - Ordered that the Court be adjourned till the second Tuesday in October next
- The Minutes of these Proceedings were signed
" JAS: HAMILTON "

- At a Court held for Loudoun County at the Courthouse of the said County on Tuesday the Thirteenth day of October in the first year of the Reign of our Sovereign Lord George the Third by the grace of God of Great Britain France and Ireland, King, Defender of the faith, &c., Anno Domini one thousand seven hundred and sixty one; Before his Majesty's Justices of the Peace for the said County, to wit;

NICHOLAS MINOR   JOHN MUCKLEHANEY &
CHARLES TYLER   BENJAMIN GRAYSON   Gent.

- An Indenture of Feofment between NICHOLAS MINOR of the one part and JOHN URQUIRT of the other part and the Memorandum of Livery of Seisen thereon endorsed were acknowledged by the said NICHOLAS and ordered to be recorded
- Dick and Tom, Negroes belonging to JEREMIAH HUTCHISON, are adjudged by the Court, Dick to be ten years and Tom to ten years of age
- Chloe, a Negro girl belonging to WALTER WILLIAMS, is adjudged by the Court to be ten years of age
- Will, a Negro boy belonging to THOMAS WILLIAMS, is adjudged by the Court to be eight years of age
- Sambo, a Negro boy, and Esther, a Negro girl, belonging to JEREMIAH COCKRILL are adjudged by the Court, Sambo to be ten years and Esther to be twelve years of age
- Indentures of Lease and Release between THOMAS CLEMSON and ELIZA-BETH his Wife of one part and JOHN HOPKINS of the other part and the Receipt thereon endorsed were acknowledged by the said THOMAS and ELIZABETH, she having been first privily examined as the Law directs, and ordered to be recorded
- Ordered that WILLIAM PEARL be appointed Surveyor of the Road in the room of WILLIAM WEST, JUNR., who is discharged from that Office
- Ordered that JAMES GOULDING be added to the List of Tithables taken for this County this present year
- Ordered that GEORGE VANDIVIER be added to the List of Tithables taken for this County this present year
- Ordered that RICHARD TRENARY be added to the List of Tithables taken for this County this present year
- Present. GEORGE WEST, Gent.
- Indentures of Lease and Release between JONAS POTTS, Blacksmith, and MARY his Wife of one part and JOHN POTTS, Farmer, of other part and the Receipt thereon endorsed were acknowledged by the said JONAS POTTS, Blacksmith, and MARY his Wife, she having been first privily examined as the Law directs, and ordered to be recorded

p.   Loudoun County Court 13th of October 1761
526   - CHARLES TYLER, Guardian of HENRY HERYFORD, is discharged from
         rendering any further Account of his Estate for the future, he being of lawful
age
- An Indenture of Lease for Lives between THOMSON MASON, Esqr., of the one part and JAMES SAUNDERS of the other part was proved by the Oaths of DAVID SMITH and NATHANIEL SMITH, witnesses thereto

- The Proceedings taken and returned against JOHN DAVIS, an ORDINARY KEEPER, for suffering unlawful gaming in his House, is continued till next Court at the motion and costs of said JOHN

- JAMES VESSELL who stand bound by Recognizance to appear here this day to answer the complaint of CHARLES COLE, Labourer, against him for Breach of the Peace, appeared according to his Recognizance and CHARLES COLE failing to appear, it is considered by the Court that JAMES VESSELL be discharged from his Recognizance and that the Complaint be dismissed

- A Bill of Sale from THOMAS PHILLIPS to ANDREW ADAM was proved by the Oaths of WILLIAM WEST and NICHOLAS MINOR, Gent., the witnesses thereto and ordered to be recorded

- An Indenture of Feofment between NICHOLAS MINOR of the one part and JOHN DAVIS of the other part and the Memorandum of Livery of Seisen thereon endorsed were acknowledged by the said NICHOLAS and ordered to be recorded

- THOMAS PHILLIPS, Plt. agt. JOHN VOILL, Deft.   In Debt
This suit is dismissed, being agreed by the parties

- JAMES WILLSON, Plt. agt. THOMAS ROGERS, Deft.   In Case
Discontinued, Plt. not further prosecuting

- JOHN CARGYLE Plt. agt. FRANCIS BALLENGER, Deft.
In Trespass Assault and Battery
The Deft. being returned not found, on motion of Plaintif an Alias Capias is awarded him returnable here at next Court

- CRAVEN PEYTON, Plt. agt. JOHN PHILLIPS, Deft.   In Case
The Deft. being returned not found, on motion of Plt.'s Attorney an Alias Capias is awarded him returnable here at next Court

p.   Loudoun County Court 13th of October 1761
527   - ANDREW ADAM, Plt. agt. STEPHEN EMRIE, Deft. In Debt
Discontinued, Plt. not further prosecuting

- Upon the Proceedings taken and returned against CHARLES COLE who stands charged with felonious stealing one Earthern Stone or Delph Mug of the value of one shillings and one glass pocket bottle of the value of ten pence current money, the property of JAMES VESSELL, CHARLES COLE appeared according to his recognizance and thereupon JAMES VESSELL being sworn and examined on behalf of our Sovereign Lord the King and CHARLES COLE heard in his own defence, On consideration whereof, it is the opinion of the Court that CHARLES COLE is Not Guilty of the Felony aforesaid and it is ordered that said CHARLES be discharged from his Recognizance aforesaid and that the Prosecution be dismissed

- Ordered that HENRY BREWER be appointed Surveyor of the Road in the room of SAMPSON TRAMMELL, who is discharged from that Office

- EDWARD GARRET, Guardian of JOHN GARRET, is excused from rendering an Account of the Profits of his Orphan's Estate till the next year

- Ordered that the Court be adjourned till the second Tuesday in November next

- The Minutes of these Proceedings were signed
                              " NICH: MINOR "

- At a Court held for Loudoun County on Monday the Ninth day of November one thousand seven hundred and sixty one for the Examination of CHARLES COLE on Suspicion of his being Guilty of stealing a Great Coat, the property of WILLIAM DODD, one fine shirt, the property of WILLIAM BAKER, one handkerchief the property of JOHN HERYFORD, one handkerchief the property of JAMES VESSELL, one Great Coat the property of JOHN MOSS, two handkerchiefs the property of JOHN DAVIS and one Shirt the property of JOHN DODD   Present

FIELDING TURNER   NICHOLAS MINOR
AENEAS CAMPBELL   GEORGE WEST   and
FRANCIS PEYTON   Gent

CHARLES COLE was set to the Bar and it being demanded of him whether he was Guilty of the felonies aforesaid or not, he said he was not thereof Guilty and thereupon WILLIAM DODD, MARGARET HERYFORD, CATHARINE DODD, ROBERT SILWOOD, SARAH VESSELL, JOHN THOMAS, JOHN CHILES, BENJAMIN HISKET and JOHN MOSS were sworn and examined as witnesses against him and he heard in his defence. On consideration whereof, it is the opinion of the Court that CHARLES COLE is Not Guilty of the Felony but that he is Guilty of Petit Larceny in stealing a Shirt, the property of JOHN DODD, and a handkerchief the property of JOHN HERYFORD of the value of eleven pence, and it is ordered that he remain in custody of the

p.   Loudoun County called Court 9th of November 1761
528   Sherif until he give Security for himself in twenty pounds and his Security in ten pounds for CHARLES COLE's personal appearance here at the next Grand Jury Court to be held for this County then and there to answer an Indictment to be exhibited against him for the said Offences. Whereupon CHARLES COLE submitted himself to the Judgment of the Justices now sitting to inflict upon him any Fine or Punishment that the Justices should think proper. Therefore it is considered by the Justices that he receive at the Public Whiping Post ten lashes on his bare back well laid on and stand in the Pillory ten minutes, and it is commanded the Sherif that he cause immediate execution thereof to be done and nothing further appearing against him, it is ordered that he be then discharged out of custody without costs
- The Minutes of these Proceedings were signed
                    " FIELDING TURNER "

- At a Court held for Loudoun County at the Courthouse on Tuesday the Tenth day of November in the Second year of the Reign of our Sovereign Lord George the Third by the grace of God of Great Britain France and Ireland, King, Defender of the faither, &c., Anno Domini one thousand seven hundred and sixty one; Before his Majesty's Justices of the Peace for the said County, to wit;
AENEAS CAMPBELL   GEORGE WEST &
NICHOLAS MINOR   FRANCIS PEYTON,   Gent.

- An Indenture of Feofment between CHARLES LITTLE JOHN, SAMUEL LITTLE JOHN and HENRY LITTLE JOHN of one part and SAMUEL IDEN of the

other part and the Memorandum of Livery of Seisen and Receipt thereon endorsed
were proved by the Oaths of STEPHEN EMREY, JAMES GILLELAND and BEN-
JAMIN HARRISS, the witnesses thereto, and ordered to be recorded

- Indentures of Lease and Release between WILLIAM ELLZEY and ALICE
his Wife of the one part and JOHN SASSER of the other part and the Receipt thereunder written were acknowledged by said WILLIAM and together with a Commission
for taking the acknowledgment and privy examination of said ALICE, and the Certificate of the execution thereof, ordered to be recorded

- Indentures of Lease and Release between WILLIAM ELLZEY and ALICE
his Wife of the one part and JOHN CARGILE of the other part and the Receipt thereunder written were acknowledged by said WILLIAM and together with a Commission
for taking the acknowledgment and privy examination of said ALICE, and the Certificate of the execution thereof, ordered to be recorded

p.   Loudoun County Court 10th of November 1761
529   - Indentures of Lease and Release between WILLIAM ELLZEY and ALICE
his Wife of one part and RICHARD KEEN of other part and the Receipt thereunder written were acknowledged by said WILLIAM and together with a Commission
for taking the acknowledgment and privy examination of said ALICE, and the Certificate of the execution thereof, ordered to be recorded

- An Indenture of Gift between RICHARD ROBERTS of the one part and
JOSEPH ROBERTS, Son of said RICHARD ROBERTS, of other part and the Memo-
randum of the Livery of Seisen thereon endorsed were proved by the Oath of LEE
MASSEY and by the Affirmation of JAMES STEERE and JOHN STEERE
(Quakers) the witnesses thereto, and ordered to be recorded

- Indentures of Lease and Release between BRYANT FAIRFAX, Esqr., of one
part and RICHARD WHITE of other part and the Receipt thereon endorsed were
proved by the Oaths of SAMUEL MEAD and GILBERT SIMPSON and by the Affirmation of SOLOMON HOGE (a Quaker) the witnesses thereto, and ordered to be
recorded

- An Indenture of Lease for Lives between BRYANT FAIRFAX, Gent., of one
part and SOLOMON HOGE of the other part was proved by the Oaths of SAMUEL
MEAD, GILBERT SIMPSON and RICHARD WHITE, witnesses thereto, and
ordered to be recorded

- Indentures of Lease and Release between BRYANT FAIRFAX, Esqr. of one
part and SAMUEL COOMBS of other part and Receipt thereon endorsed were proved
by the Oaths of SAMUEL MEAD, GILBERT SIMPSON and by the Affirmation of
SOLOMON HOGE (a Quaker) the witnesses thereto, and ordered to be recorded

- Indentures of Lease and Release between BRYANT FAIRFAX, Esqr. of one
part and SAMUEL WILKS of other part and Receipt thereon endorsed were proved
by the Oaths of SAMUEL MEAD and GILBERT SIMPSON and by the Affirmation
of SOLOMON HOGE (a Quaker) the witnesses thereto, and ordered to be recorded

- Present. FIELDING TURNER and RICHARD COLEMAN, Gent.

- The Last Will and Testament of JOSEPH YATES, deced., was proved by the
Affirmation of FRANCIS HAGUE, THOMAS LAMB and WILLIAM WILDMAN
(Quakers) witnesses thereto and is ordered to be recorded; And on motion of ALICE
YATES and ISRAEL THOMPSON, the Executors therein named, who affirmed

according to Law, Certificate is granted them for obtaining a Probat thereof in due form giving security; Whereupon they together with FRANCIS HAGUE and THO-MAS LAMB, their Securities, entered into and acknowledged Bond in the Penalty of one thousand pounds with conditon as the Law directs

p.   Loudoun County Court 10th of November 1761
530   - Ordered that WILLIAM WILDMAN, MAHLON JANNEY, ABEL JAN-
        NEY and THOMAS GORE or any three of them being first sworn before a
Justice of this County, do appraise in current money the slaves (if any) and personal
Estate of JOSEPH YATES, deced., and return the Appraisment to the Court
        - The Sheriff having returned a Panel of the Grand Jury, to wit;

JOHN CARLYLE	THOMAS OWSLEY	BENJAMIN MASON
JOSHUA GORE, JUNR.	JACOB REMEY	HENRY WISHEART
THOMAS SORRELL	JOHN MOSS	HENRY MOORE
HENRY TAYLOR	OWEN ROBERTS	JOHN HALL
JOHN SMARR	ELIJAH CHINN	THOMAS CONNELL
FRANCIS SUMMERS	GEORGE HEADEN and	WILLIAM TRAMMELL

Freeholders of County of Loudoun to serve as a Grand Jury for said County at this Court, who being solemnly called, the following persons so summoned did not appear, vizt.

VINCENT LEWIS	HENRY WISHEART	JOHN MOSS
HENRY MOORE	OWEN ROBERTS	SAMUEL COMPTON
EDWARD GARRETT	JOHN HUTCHISON	WALTER WILLIAMS
ELIJAH CHINN	FRANCIS SUMMERS and	GEORGE HEADEN

by means whereof fifteen Freeholders did not appear so that no Grand Jury could be sworn, ordered that each of the above persons, to wit,

VINCENT LEWIS	HENRY WISHEART	JOHN MOSS
HENRY MOORE	OWEN ROBERTS	SAMUEL COMPTON
EDWARD GARRETT	JOHN HUTCHISON	WALTER WILLIAMS
ELIJAH CHINN	FRANCIS SUMMERS and	GEORGE HEADEN

be Fined four hundred pounds of tobacco to the King, his heirs and successors to the use of the said County unless each or any of them shew sufficient cause why Judg-ment shou'd not be entered against them at the next Court.
        - An Indenture of Feofment between JOHN NEWTON, Gent., and BETTY his Wife of one part and WILLIAM CARR LANE of other part and the Memorandum of Livery of Seisen and Receipt thereon endorsed , also a Bond for performance of Cove-nants, from JOHN NEWTON to WILLIAM CARR LANE were proved by the Oath of WILLIAM CARR TIDWELL, a witness thereto
        - An Indenture of Lease for Lives between THOMPSON MASON, Esqr., of one part and JAMES SANDERS of other part was proved by the Oath of ABRAHAM WEAVER, a witness thereto, and the same having been before proved by the Oaths of NATHANIEL SMITH and DAVID SMITH, witnesses thereto, is ordered to be recorded
        - Ordered that the Court be adjourned till tomorrow morning eight o'clock
        - The Minutes of these Proceedings were signed
                                        " FIELDING TURNER "

p.   - At a Court continued and held for Loudoun County at the Courthouse on
531   Wednesday the Eleventh day of November one thousand seven hundred and
        sixty one; Before his Majesty's Justices of the Peace for said County, to wit;

FIELDING TURNER   NICHOLAS MINOR &
AENEAS CAMPBELL   FRANCIS PEYTON   Gent.

- WILLIAM GRANT on his motion is by the Court discharged from the paiment of Levies and Poll Tax for the future

- Ordered that Licence be granted unto HENRY MOORE to keep ORDINARY at his House on ROCKEY RUN in this County for one year, he with FRANCIS PEYTON and CHARLES BINNS, his Securities, having entered into Bond as the Law directs

- Present. RICHARD COLEMAN, Gent.

- Upon the Proceedings taken and returned against JOHN WELLS who stands charged with the felonious stealing two narrow axes and two drawing knives, the property of JOHN TRAMMELL, said JOHN WELLS appeared according to his Recognizance and it being demanded of him whether he was Guilty of the Felony aforesaid or not, he said he was Not thereof Guilty, and thereupon JOHN TRAMMELL, WILLIAM TRAMMELL, SAMUEL PATTERSON, THOMAS PHILLIPS and PATRICK McKINZEY were sworn and examined as witnesses against him and he heard in his defence; On consideration whereof, it is the opinion of the Court that he is Not Guilty of Felony but that he is Guilty of a misdemeanor, and it is ordered that he enter into Recognizance in the sum of ten pounds for his good behavior for the space of one year from this time, And thereupon JOHN WELLS came into Court and acknowledged himself indebted to our Sovereign Lord George the Third, King of Great Britain, &c., in the sum of ten pounds of his lands and tenements goods and chattels to be levied and to our Lord the King his heirs and successors rendered, Yet upon condition that if JOHN WELLS shall be of good behavior towards the King and all his liege People for the space of one year as aforesaid, then this Recognizance to be void

- WILLIAM FLOYD, Infant, Orphan of JOHN FLOYD, deceased, with the approbation of the Court made choice of WILLIAM ELLZEY, Gent., for his Guardian who together with LEE MASSEY, his Security, entered into and acknowledged Bond as the Law directs, which Bond is ordered to be recorded

- On motion of WILLIAM ADAMS, Exr. of GABRIEL ADAMS, deced., it is ordered that RICHARD COLEMAN, Gent., JAMES COLEMAN, WILLIAM LITTLETON and WILLIAM STARK or any three thereof allot and assign ELIZABETH ADAMS's Dower in her late Husband, GABRIEL ADAMS's, deced., Estate and make report thereof to the Court

- The Petition of WILLIAM DODD against JOHN OWSLEY is dismissed, being agreed between the parties, and it is ordered that Deft. pay unto Plt. his costs

- Ordered that DANIEL NEALE be added to the List of Tithables taken for this County this present year

p.   Loudoun County Court 11th of November 1761
532   - WILLIAM GOSSETT, HUGH KERRIGIN, JOHN BALL, MICHAEL
         BUSCART, WILLIAM BLACK, ABNER HOWELL and GRIFFY MATTHIAS
who stood bound by Recognizance to appear here this day to answer the Complaint of PHILIP LYNHAM against them for Breach of the Peace, appeared accordingly; Whereupon WILLIAM GOSSETT, HUGH KERRIGIN, JOHN BALL, MICHAEL BUSCART, WILLIAM BLACK, ABNER HOWELL and GRIFFY MATTHIAS and

said PHILIP LYNHAM were fully heard and divers witnesses examined touching the matter of Complaint; On consideration whereof it is ordered that WILLIAM GOS-SETT, HUGH KERRIGIN, JOHN BALL, MICHAEL BUSCART, WILLIAM BLACK, ABNER HOWELL and GRIFFY MATTHIAS be discharged from their Recognizance aforesaid and that the Complaint be dismissed

- JAMES ABBETT, an Evidence for RICHARD COLEMAN, Gent., against OWEN ROBERTS having attended Court seven days, ordered said RICHARD pay him one hundred seventy five pounds of tobacco for the same

- Ordered that the Churchwardens of Cameron Parish bind out MARY McNAB a base born Child two years old the 13th of this instant November to JOHN CARR according to Law

- An Indenture of Feofment between NICHOLAS MINOR, Gent., of one part and JOHN MEGINNIS of other part and the Memorandum of Livery of Seisin thereon endorsed were acknowledged by said NICHOLAS and ordered to be recorded

- JOHN STONE, Plt. agt. JOHN PALMER, DANIEL PALMER and
  THOMAS PALMER, Defts.   In Trespass
This suit is dismissed, being agreed by the parties

- Ordered that THOMAS AWBREY and his two Tithables, to wit, Negroes Butcher and Bill be added to the List of Tithables taken for this County this present year

- ANDREW ADAM, Plt. agt. THOMAS PHILLIPS, Deft.   In Debt
This suit is dismissed, being agreed by the parties

- ROBERT POPKINS, Plt. agt. JOHN PHILLIPS, Deft.   In Case
The Deft. being again returned not found, on motion of Plt.'s Attorney a Plurius Capias is awarded him returnable here at next Court

- An Indenture of Feofment between NICHOLAS MINOR, Gent., of one part and CRAVEN PEYTON of other part and Receipt and Memorandum of Livery of Seisin thereon endorsed were acknowledged by said NICHOLAS and is ordered to be recorded

p   Loudoun County Court 11th of November 1761
533   - The Court proceeded to lay and assess the Levy for this County as follows;

	lbs. tobacco
Mr. Secretary NELSON as pr. Account	360
WILLIAM WEST present Sherif for Public Services and Cask	1248
ditto as pr Account	516
AENEAS CAMPBELL, Gent., as pr. Account L. 3..15..0 in tobacco	
at 12/6 p ct.	600
CHARLES BINNS, Clerk, for Public Services and Cask	1248
ditto as pr Account	1040
ditto ditto for 2 Record Books and paying WAGENER	
for bringing the same 45/, in tobacco	360
HUGH WEST, Gent. Deputy Attorney as Salary	2000
ditto as pr Account	400
BENJAMIN SEBASTIAN for 2 Levies overcharged last year 6 lbs. tobo. each	12
JAMES LEITH as pr Account proved	25
NICHOLAS MINOR, Gent., late Sherif as pr Account	352
WILLIAM ALLAN for 1 Levy overcharged last year	6
GEORGE ALLAN for 2 ditto ditto	12
JOHN ALLAN for 1 ditto ditto	6

JOSEPH WEST for Halling Stone & Underpinning the Prison
L. 10. in tobo. @ 12/6 p ct. is   1600
JOHN MOSS, JUNR., for his services in finding wood, water & cleaning
the Courthouse, &c.   1000
JOHN TRAMELL as pr Agreement for keeping BROAD RUN BRIDGE in
repair seven years   7120
                                                                            17905

Loudoun County	Dr. lbs. tobacco
Amount of several claims	17905
Depositum in the hands of the Sherif	2939
6 p ct. for collecting 20,844 lbs. tobacco	1331
	22175

pr. Contra	Cr. lbs. tobacco
By 1479 Tithables @ 15 lbs. tobacco pr Poll is	22175

- Ordered that the Sherif collect from every Tithable Person in this County fifteen pounds of tobacco according to the above Levy this day assessed
- Ordered that the hands at the Quarter where NICHOLAS WREN is Overseer belonging to FRANCIS LIGHTFOOT LEE, Gent., and the hands at BRAY's Quarter be discharged from working on the Road whereof JAMES WHALEY is Surveyor and that they work on the Road whereof ANTHONY RUSSELL, Gent., is Surveyor
- An Indenture of Assignment between WILLIAM HANCOCK of one part and DANIEL NEAL of other part was acknowledged by said WILLIAM and is ordered to be recorded
- Ordered that the Court be adjourned till tomorrow morning eight o'clock
- The Minutes of these Proceedings were signed
                                " FIELDING TURNER "

p.   - At a Court continued and held for Loudoun County at the Courthouse on
534   Thursday the Twelfth day of November one thousand seven hundred and sixty
       one, Before his Majesty's Justices of the Peace for said County, to wit;
              FIELDING TURNER   RICHARD COLEMAN
              NICHOLAS MINOR   JOSIAS CLAPHAM   &
                     FRANCIS PEYTON   Gent.

- THOMAS HARRISON, JAMES NISBET, BENJAMIN GRAYSON and SPENCE GRAYSON, Exrs. of the Last Will and Testament of BENJAMIN GRAYSON, Gent., deced., Plts. agt. JOHN KING, Deft.   In Case
Continued till next Court at motion and costs of Plts.
- FRANCIS PEYTON and NICHOLAS MINOR, Gent., Churchwardens for the time being for the Parish of Cameron in the County of Loudoun, Plts. agt. ANN GRIFFIN, Deft.   In Debt
The Deft. being arrested and not appearing, on motion of Plts. by HUGH WEST, their Attorney, it is ordered that unless Deft. shall appear here at next Court and answer the action of Plts., Judgment shall thenbe given for Plts. against her for the

Debt in the Declaration mentioned and costs
        - REBECCA EADES, an Infant under the age of twenty one years by THO-
        MAS PHILLIPS, her Guardian and next Friend, Plt. agt. JOHN LACKEY
        and JACOB GARDNER, Defts.   In Trespass Assault and Battery
    The Deft., JACOB, by WILLIAM ELLZEY his Attorney saving to himself all ad-
vantages of Exceptions as well to Plt.'s Writ as to her Declaration, prays and has
leave to imparl till next Court and then to plead
        - BENJAMIN GRAYSON and STACEY his Wife, Admrx. of BURGESS
        BERKLEY, deced., Complts. agt. WILLIAM BERKLEY, Deft.   In Chancery
    The Deft. filed and answer which Complts. have time till next Court to reply
        - WILLIAM GOSSETT, JUNR., Plt. agt. SAMUEL DAVIS, JUNR., Deft.
        In Trespass Assault and Battery
    The Deft. being again returned not to be found, on motion of Plt.'s Attorney, a
Plurius Capias is awarded him returnable here at next Court

p.   Loudoun County Court 12th of November 1761
535   - HECTOR ROSS, Plt. agt. JOHN CALLIHAM and THOMAS KELLY,
        Defts.   In Debt
    The Defts. being arrested and not appearing on motion of Plt. by WILLIAM
ELLZEY, his Attorney, it is ordered that unless Defts. shall appear here at next
Court and answer Plt.'s action, Judgment shall then be given for Plt. against them
and JOSEPH POWER, who is returned security for their appearance, for the Debt in
the Declaration mentioned
        - THOMSON MASON, Plt. agt. FRANKLIN PERRY, Deft.
        Upon a Writ of Scire
    This day came Plt. by HUGH WEST, his Attorney, and Deft. altho' solemnly called
came not. Therefore it is considered by the Court that Plt. ought to have execution
against Deft. for the sum of four pounds, five shilllings, eighty two pounds of nett
tobacco and fifteen shillings or one hundred and fifty pounds of tobacco and his costs
by him in this behalf expended and Deft. in mercy, &c.
        - WILLIAM SAUNDERS, Plt. agt. THOMAS AWBREY, Admr. of all and
        singular the goods and chattels, rights and credits of WALTER ENGLISH,
        deced., Deft.   In Chancery
    On motion of Plt. by HUGH WEST, his Attorney, time is allowed him till next Court
to file his Bill
        - WILLIAM ELLZEY, Plt. agt. JOHN ANDERSON, Deft.   In Case
    The Deft. being arrested and not appearing tho' solemnly called, on motion of Plt. it
is ordered that unless Deft. shall apear here at next Court and answer Plt.'s action,
Judgment shall then be given for Plt. against him and JOHN HERYFORD, JOHN
CARGYLE and JOHN OWSLEY, who were returned Securities for his appearance,
for his damages and costs
        - SIMON PEARSON and MILKEY PEARSON, his Wife, Complts. agt.
        JOHN TRAMMELL and SAMPSON TRAMMELL, Exrs. of the Last Will and
        Testament of JOHN TRAMMELL, deced., Defts.   In Chancery
    This day came Plts. by their Attorney and Defendants having failed to answer the
Bill of the Plts., it is ordered that the same be taken as confessed and the matter of
Equity therein in be decreed unless Defts. do answer the same at next Court

p.   Loudoun County Court 12th of November 1761
536   - SARAH LEWIS, Widow and Relict of THOMAS LEWIS, deced., Complt.
       agt. WILLIAM DOUGLASS and ELIZABETH his Wife, late ELIZABETH
       LEWIS, Defts.   In Chancery
The Defendant ELIZABETH filed an answer which Complt. has time till next Court
to reply
       - SIMON PEARSON and MILKEY PEARSON his Wife, WILLIAM STARKE
       and SUSANNA STARKE his Wife, EZEKIEL HICKMAN and ELIZABETH
       his Wife and WILLIAM TRAMMELL, Plts. agt. JOHN TRAMMELL and
       SAMPSON TRAMMELL Defts.   In Chancery
The Deft. filed an answer which Complts. have time till next Court to reply
       - JOHN CARGYLE, Plt. agt. FRANCIS BALLENGER, Deft.
       In Trespass Assault and Battery
Discontinued, the Plt. not further prosecuting
       - CRAVEN PEYTON, Plt. agt. JOHN PHILLIPS, Deft.   In Case
The Deft. being again return not to be found, on motion of Plt.'s Attorney a Plurius
Capias is awarded him returnable here at next Court
       - Upon Petition of ROBERT MITCHELL against ISRAEL THOMPSON for a
Debt due by Account, This day came the parties by their Attornies, who being fully
heard, it is considered by the Court that Plt. recover against Deft. two pounds, two
shillings and six pence and his costs by him in this behalf expended, including seven
shillings and six pence for a Lawyer's fee
       - WILLIAM LUCKETT, an Evidence for ROBERT MITCHELL against
ISRAEL THOMPSON having attended Court three daies, ordered that said ROBERT
pay in seventy five pounds of tobacco for the same
       - An Indenture of Feofment between ANDREW LINK of one part and THO-
MAS PRITCHARD of other part and the Memorandum of Livery of Seisen and Receipt thereunder written were proved by the Oaths of JOHN DAVIS, WILLIAM
BAKER and JOHN URQUHART, witnesses thereto, and ordered to be recorded
       - JOHN DAVIS, Plt. agt. ELIZABETH LEWIS, Deft.   In Case
Continued till next Court by consent of the parties

p.   Loudoun County Court 12th of November 1761
537   - GEORGE HEADEN, Plt. agt. JOHN CAIN, Deft.   In Debt
       Continued till next Court at motion and costs of Deft.
       - THOMAS HARRISON, JAMES NISBET, BENJAMIN GRAYSON and
       SPENCE GRAYSON, Exrs. of the Last Will and Testament of BENJAMIN
       GRAYSON, Gent., deced., Plts. against GEORGE HANCOCKE, Deft. In Case
Continued till next Court at motion and costs of Plts.
       - THOMAS BULLITT, Plt. agt. CHARLES LEWIS, Deft.   In Case
Continued till next Court at motion and costs of Plt.
       - Aminidab Goodtitle, Lessee of JOHN WATSON, Plt. agt. Ferdinando Bad-
       title, Deft.   In Ejectment for one messuage and one hundred fifty acres of land
       with appurtenances lying and being in Parish of Cameron and County of Lou-
       doun
Continued till next Court at motion and costs of Plt.

- JOHN DAVIS & MARGARET his Wife, late MARGARET DAVIS, Admrx. &c. of THOMAS DAVIS, the Elder, deceased, Plts. agt. ELIZABETH DAVIS Admrx. &c. of THOMAS DAVIS, the Younger, deced., Deft.   In Case
Continued till next Court at motion and costs of Plts.
- HENRY PEYTON, Gent., Plt. agt. SAMUEL STILLWELL, Deft. In Case
Continued till next Court at motion and costs of Plt.
- JOSIAS CLAPHAM, Gent., Plt. agt. EZEKIEL HICKMAN, Deft.   In Case
Continued till next Court by consent of the parties
- THOMAS MOXLEY, Plt. agt. JOHN TRAMMELL, Deft.   In Case
Continued till next Court at motion and costs of Plt.
- HUGH WEST, Plt. agt. RODHAM NEALE, Deft.   In Case
Continued till next Court at motion and costs of Deft.

p.   Loudoun County Court 12th of November 1761
538   - BENJAMIN EDWARDS, Plt. agt. JAMES LAYTON, Admr. &c. of WILLIAM LAYTON, deced., Deft.   In Covenant
Continued till next Court at motion and costs of Deft.
- CHARLES COLE, Plt. agt. HUGH FOUCH, Deft.
In Trespass, Assault and Battery
Continued till next Court by consent of the parties

- Upon the Petition of   SAMUEL MEAD   SOLOMON HOGE
WILLIAM WILDMAN   WILLIAM HATCHER   WILLIAM DODD
THOMAS FIELD   FRANCIS WILKS   SAMUEL WILKS
JOHN SIMS   ROBERT STUKESBURY ISAAC NICHOLS and
BENJAMIN POOLE   praying that a Road may be opened from JACOB JANNEY's to ANDREW ADAM's Mill on SEKELON; It is ordered that WILLIAM MEAD, WILLIAM ROSS, JOHN MOSS and THOMAS SORRELL or any three thereof being first sworn before a Justice of this County, do view the most convenient way for the same and make report of the conveniency and inconveniency that will attend the same to the Court
- An Indenture of Feofment between NICHOLAS MINOR of one part and JAMES VESSELLS of other part and Memorandum of Livery of Seisin thereon endorsed were acknowledged by NICHOLAS MINOR and ordered to be recorded
- MARY JORDAN, Plt. agt. LEROY HUGHLETT, Deft.   In Case
Continued till next Court at motion and costs of Plt.
- JAMES INGOE DOZER, Plt. agt. JAMES McKINNEY, Deft.   In Debt
Continued till next Court at motion and costs of Deft.
- BENJAMIN GRAYSON, Mercht., Plt. agt. WILLIAM HARDY, Deft. In Case
Continued till next Court at motion and costs of Plt.
- JOHN HERRYFORD, Plt. agt. JOSEPH STEPHENS, Deft.
In Trespass Assault and Battery
Continued till next Court at motion and costs of Deft.
- JOHN GODDARD, Plt. agt. HENRY WISHEART, Deft.
In Trespass Assault and Battery
Continued till next Court at motion and costs of Deft.

p.   Loudoun County Court 12th of November 1761
539   EZEKIEL HICKMAN, Plt. agt. THOMAS AWBREY, Deft.

Upon a Writ of Scire Facias

This day came the parties by their Attornies and Deft. relinquishing his former Plea saith that he cannot gainsay Plt.'s action. Therefore by consent of the parties, it is considered by the Court that Plt. ought to have execution against Deft. for sum of twelve hundred pounds of tobacco, five hundred thirty three pounds of nett tobacco and fifteen shillings or one hundred and fifty pounds of tobacco and his costs by him in this behalf expended and the Deft. in mercy, &c.

- JOHN GODDARD, Plt. agt. SAMPSON TURLEY, Deft.

In Trespass Assault and Battery

Continued till next Court at motion and costs of Plt.

- WILLIAM DODD, Plt. agt. JOHN RICHARDS, Deft.   In Debt

Continued till next Court at motion and costs of Deft.

- WILLIAM DOUGLASS and ELIZABETH DOUGLASS his Wife, Plts. agt. EZEKIEL HICKMAN, Deft.   In Case

Continued till next Court at motion and costs of Plts.

- The Information of NICHOLAS MINOR and JAMES LANE, Gent., Church-wardens for the Parish of Cameron against JAMES COLEMAN and JANE his Wife is discontinued, the Plts. not prosecuting

- Ordered that other Process issue against BENJAMIN GRAYSON, Guardian of WILLIAM GRAYSON, and FRANCIS HAGUE, Guardian of WILLIAM SHORES, who ought to have rendered their Accounts to the Court and have failed therein returnable here at next Court to compel them to render such Accounts at that time

- JOHN HALL, Guardian of SUSANNA HALL and MARY HALL, having been duly summoned to render Accounts of the Profits of their Estates to the Court and failing to do the same, it is ordered that an Attachment issue against him for his contempt returnable here at next Court

- ANDREW ADAM, Mercht., Plt. agt. JAMES GOULDING, Deft.   In Case

JOHN ANDERSON of this County comes into Court and undertakes for Deft. that in case

p.   Loudoun County Court 12th of November 1761
540   he shall be cast in this suit he shall pay and satisfy the condemnation of the
        Court or render his body to Prison in execution for the same or that he, the said JOHN, will do it for him; And Deft., by WILLIAM ELLZEY, his Attorney, saving to himself all advantages of Exceptions as well to Plt.'s Writ as to his Declaration, prays and has leave to imparl till next Court and then to plead

- JAMES HOOK, Complt. agt. JOSEPH CLAYPOOL, Deft.   In Chancery

On motion of Complt. by WILLIAM ELLZEY, his Attorney, time is allowed him till next Court to file his Bill

- BENJAMIN LADD, Plt. agt. JOHN RICHARDS, Deft.   In Debt

Discontinued, the Plt. not further prosecuting

- ANDREW ADAM, Plt. agt. JOSEPH JEANY, Deft.   In Case

This day came the parties by their Attornies and Deft. saving to himself all advantages of Exceptions as well to Plt.'s Writ as to his Declaraton, prays and has leave to imparl till next Court and then to plead

- CRAVEN PEYTON, Gent., Plt. agt. JONATHAN MONKHOUSE, Deft.

In Trespass

By Agreement of the parties this suit is dismissed and it is ordered that Deft. pay unto Plt. his costs

    - CHARLES COLE, Plt. agt. JAMES VESSELS, Deft.
    In Trespass Assault and Battery

This suit is dismissed, being agreed by the parties

    - CRAVEN PEYTON, Plt. agt. DANIEL McGINNIS, Deft.   In Case

This day came as well Plt. by HUGH WEST his Attorney as Deft. in custody of WILLIAM WEST, Gent., Sherif of this County, and Deft. acknowledged Plt.'s action for eleven pounds, three shillings and four pence. Therefore it is considered by the Court that Plt. recover against Deft. the eleven pounds, three shilliings and four pence and his costs by him in this behalf expended and the Deft. in mercy, &c.

p.   Loudoun County Court 12th of November 1761
541   - CRAVEN PEYTON, Plt. agt. JOHN ROSS DEWITT otherwise called I
      JOHN ROSS DEWITT of Loudoun County, Planter, Deft.   In Debt

The Deft. being arrested and not appearing altho' solemnly called, on motion of Plt. by HUGH WEST, his Attorney, it is ordered that unless Deft. shall appear here at next Court and answer Plt.'s action, Judgment shall then be given for Plt. against Deft. and WILLIAM ROSS, who is returned Security for his appearance, for the Debt in the Declaration mentioned and costs

    - CRAVEN PEYTON, Plt. agt. JOHN OWSLEY, otherwise called I JOHN
      OWSLEY of Loudoun County, Planter, Deft.   In Debt

The Deft. being arrested and not appearing altho' solemnly called, on motion of Plt. by HUGH WEST, his Attorney, it is ordered that unless Deft. shall appear here at next Court and answer Plt.'s action, Judgment shall then be given for Plt. against Deft. and ROBERT STEVENS, who is returned Security for his appearance, for the Debt in the Declaration mentioned and costs

    - NICHOLAS MINOR, Plt. agt. HENRY PEYTON, Deft.   In Debt

The Deft. being arrested and not appearing altho' solemnly called, on motion of Plt. by HUGH WEST, his Attorney, it is ordered that unless Deft. shall appear here at next Court and answer Plt.'s action, Judgment shall then be given for Plt. against Deft. and LEVEN POWELL, who is returned Security for his appearance, for the Debt in the Declaration mentioned and costs

    - AENEAS CAMPBELL, Assignee of GEORGE MAXWELL and JAMES
      FORBES, Plt., agt. JAMES VESSELLLS, Deft.   In Debt

The Deft. being arrested and not appearing altho' solemnly called, on motion of Plt. by HUGH WEST, his Attorney, it is ordered that unless Deft. shall appear here at next Court and answer Plt.'s action, Judgment shall then be given for Plt. against Deft. and THOMAS PRITCHARD, who is returned Security for his appearance, for the Debt in the Declaration mentioned and costs

    - AENEAS CAMPBELL, Gent., Plt. agt. ROBERT WOOD, Deft.   In Case

The Deft. being arrested and not appearing altho' solemnly called, on motion of Plt. by HUGH WEST, his Attorney, it is ordered that unless Deft. shall appear here at next Court and answer

p.   Loudoun County Court 12th of November 1761
542   Plt.'s action, Judgment shall then be given for Plt. against Deft. and JAMES

LEITH, who is returned Security for his appearance, for his damages and costs
            - JONATHAN DAVIS, Plt. agt. WILLIAM CONNELL, Deft.   In Debt
This day came the parties by their Attornies and Deft. saving to himself all advantages of Exceptions as well to Plt.'s Writ as to his Declaration, prays and has leave to
imparl till next Court and then to plead
            - THOMAS PRITCHARD, Plt. agt. SILL ADDAMS, Deft.   In Debt
This day came the parties by their Attornies and Deft. saving to himself all advantages of Execptions as well to Plt.'s Writ as to his Declaration, prays and has leave to
imparl till next Court and then to plead
            - JOHN NEWTON, Gent., Assignee of WILLOUGHBY NEWTON, Gent., Plt.
            agt. JOHN MORRIS, Deft.   In Debt
This day came the parties by their Attornies and Deft. saving to himself all advan-
ages of Exceptions as well to Plt.'s Writ as to his Declaration, prays and has leave to
imparl till next Court and then to plead
            - ROBERT EASTHAM, Plt. agt. AARON BOTTS, Deft. Upon a Scire Facias
This day came Plt. by WILLIAM ELLZEY, his Attorney, and Deft. altho' solemnly
called came not. Therefore it is considered by the Court that Plt. ought to have execution against Deft. for sum of nine pounds, nineteen shillings and six pence half
penny current money of Virginia, three hundred forty five pounds of nett tobacco,
fifteen shillings or one hundred fifty pounds of tobacco and his costs by him in this
behalf expended and said Deft. in mercy, &c.
            - THOMAS PRITCHARD, Plt. agt. JOHN GOWERS, Deft.   In Case
This suit is dismissed being agreed by the parties
            - JOHN WINN, Plt. agt. JOHN LAMBERT, Deft.   In Case
This suit is dismissed being agreed by the parties

p.   Loudoun County Court 12th of November 1761
543   - JACOB FREDERICK CURTIUS, Plt. agt. JOHN MARTIN WINTNALE,
        Deft. In Debt.
Continued till next Court
            - Messrs. HUNTER, CAMPBELL and COMPANY, Plts. agt. THOMAS
            BLINCOE, Carpenter, Deft.   In Debt
The Deft. being arrested and not appearing altho' solemnly called, on motion of Plt.
by WILLIAM ELLZEY, his Attorney, it is ordered that unless Deft. shall appear here
at next Court and answer the action of Plts., Judgment shall then be given for Plts.
against Deft. and WILLIAM SMITH and THOMAS FIELDS, who are returned
Securities for his appearance, for the Debt in the Declaration mentioned and costs
            - ANDREW ADAMS, Plt. agt. STEPHEN EMRIE, Deft.   In Case
The Deft. being arrested and not appearing altho' solemnly called, on motion of Plt.
by HUGH WEST, his Attorney, it is ordered that unless Deft. shall appear here at
next Court and answer the action of Plt., Judgment shall then be given for Plts.
against Deft. and BENJAMIN SHACKLET and EPHRAIM HAMMON, who are returned Securities for his appearance, for his damages and costs
            - ARCHIBALD CRAWFORD, Plt. against SYLVESTER GARDNER and
            JACOB GARDNER, Defts.   In Trespass Assault and Battery
HUGH WEST in Court undertakes for Plt. that in case Plt. shall be cast in this suit
he shall pay and satisfy all such damages costs and charges as shall be awarded

against him or he will pay them for him, and the Defts. by BENJAMIN SEBASTIAN their Attorney, saving to themselves all advantages of Exceptions as well to Plt.'s Writ as to his Declaration pray and have leave to imparl till next Court and then to plead

- WILLIAM DODD, Plt. agt. THOMAS LIDDLE, Deft.   In Case

The Deft. being arrested and not appearing altho' solemnly called, on motion of Plt. by HUGH WEST, his Attorney, it is ordered that unless Deft. shall appear here at next Court and answer Plt.'s action, Judgment shall then be given for Plt. against Deft. and DANIEL JAMES, who is returned Security for his appearance, for his damages and costs

- Upon Petition of HUGH WEST against RICHARD ROBERTS for a Debt due by Account, This day came Plt. in his proper person and Deft. having been duly summoned was solemnly called but came not; Therefore it is considered by the Court that Plt. recover against Deft. one pound, seventeen shillings and six pence and his costs by him in this behalf expended

p.   <u>Loudoun County Court 12th of November 1761</u>
544   - JOHN TRAMMELL, Plt. agt. WILLIAM COLVIN, Deft.
      Upon an Attachment
JOSIAS CLAPHAM, Gent., a Garnishee, being sworn declares that he has in his hands of Deft.'s effects one Bible. It is ordered that the same remain in his hands till further Orders of this Court; And on motion of Plt.'s Attorney, the Attachment is continued till next Court for the other Garnishees to declare

- CRAVEN PEYTON, Plt. agt. WILLIAM COLVIN, Deft.
      Upon an Attachment
Continued till next Court for Garnishees to declare

- AARON RICHARDSON, Plt. agt. WILLIAM COLVIN, Deft.
      Upon an Attachment
Continued till next Court for Garnishees to declare

- JAMES WILLSON, Plt. agt. THOMAS RODGERS, Deft.
      Upon an Attachment
JOHN ANDERSON, a Garnishee, being sworn declares that he has nothing of the Deft.'s effects in his hands and thereupon is discharged and the Attachment is continued till next Court for the other Garnishee to declare

- FLEMING PATTERSON, Plt. agt. DANIEL MEGINNIS, Deft.
      Upon an Attachment
CHARLES HOLE, a Garnishee, being sworn declares he has nothing of Deft.'s effects in his hands and thereupon he is discharged, and the Attachment is discontinued, Plt. not further prosecuting

- WILLIAM DODD, Plt. agt. THOMAS LIDDLE, Deft. Upon an Attachment
Discontinued, Plt. not further prosecuting

- CRAVEN PEYTON, Plt. agt. THOMAS LIDDLE, Deft. Upon an Attachment
Continued till next Court for Garnishees to declare

- Ordered that NICHOLAS MINOR, Gent., and JOHN MOSS, JUNR. agree with Workmen to clear away the Bricks and Dirt about the Courthouse and likewise for building a Necessary House, and Posting and Railing in the Courthouse Lott and bring in their Account to the laying of the next Levy

p.   <u>Loudoun County Court 12th of November 1761</u>
545   - JOHN DAVIS, Plt. agt. NORTHROP MARPOLE, Deft.
      Upon an Attachment
This day came Plt. by HUGH WEST, his Attorney and Deft. altho' solemnly called came not. Therefore it is considered by the Court that Plt. recover against Deft. two pounds, ten shillings and his costs by him in this behalf expended, and Deft. in mercy, &c.

    AENEAS CAMPBELL, Gent., a Garnishee, confesses that he has in his hands sufficient to satisfy Plt.'s demand due by a Bond from said AENEAS to Deft. payable about the last of August next. It is ordered that said AENEAS pay Plt. his Debt and costs aforesaid after the last day of August next ensuing

    - An Account of the Administration of the Estate of SARAH DAVIS, deceased, was returned into Court by THOMAS PRITCHARD and RACHEL his Wife, the Executrix, to which said THOMAS made Oath and the same being examined and approved of by the Court is ordered to be recorded

    - Ordered the Court be adjourned till tomorrow morning eight o'clock

    - The Minutes of these Proceedings were signed
" FIELDING TURNER "

    - At a Court continued and held for Loudoun County at the Courthouse on Friday the Thirteenth day of November one thousand seven hundred and sixty one, Before his Majesty's Justices of the Peace for said County, to wit;

NICHOLAS MINOR   RICHARD COLEMAN, &
AENEAS CAMPBELL   FRANCIS PEYTON,   Gent.

    - An Indenture of Feofment between NICHOLAS MINOR, Gent., of one part and AENEAS CAMPBELL, Gent. of other part and Memorandum of Livery of Seisin and Receipt theron endorsed were acknowledged by NICHOLAS MINOR and ordered to be recorded

    - A Power of Attorney from the Right Honble. CHARLES EARL of TANKER-VILLE to JOHN PATTERSON and the Certificate of the Proof of the execution of the same before Sir RICHARD GLYN, Knight, Lord Mayor of London, under the Seal of the Office of Mayoralty of the said City was presented into Court by JOHN PATTER-SON and on his motion ordered to be recorded

    - Upon Petition of SAMUEL WINN against THOMAS LEWIS in Trover; This day came the parties by their Attornies, who being fully heard, it is considered by the Court that the Petition be dismissed and that Plt. pay unto Deft. his costs

p.   <u>Loudoun County Court 13th of November 1761</u>
546   - CHARLES CHILTON, an Evidence for THOMAS LEWIS, at the suit of
      SAMUEL WINN having attended Court four daies, ordered that THOMAS LEWIS pay him one hundred pounds of tobacco for the same

    - JACOB GARDNER, an Evidence of THOMAS LEWIS, at the suit of SAMUEL WINN, having attended Court four daies, ordered that THOMAS LEWIS pay him one hundred pounds of tobacco for the same

    - THOMAS RODEN, an Evidence for THOMAS LEWIS, at the suit of SAMUEL WINN, having attended Court four days and for travelling sixty miles from

FREDERICK County and returning, ordered that THOMAS LEWIS pay him two hundred eighty pounds of tobacco for the same

     - HENRY POLLEN, an Evidence for THOMAS LEWIS at the suit of SAMUEL WINN, having attended Court four daies, ordered that THOMAS LEWIS pay him one hundred pounds of tobacco for the same

     - Ordered that the Court be adjourned till the second Tuesday in December next

     - The Minutes of these Proceedings were signed
" AENS: CAMPBELL "

     - At a Court held for Loudoun County at the Courthouse on Tuesday the Eighth day of December in the second year of the Reign of our Sovereign Lord George the Third by the grace of God of Great Britain France and Ireland, King, Defender of the faith, &c., Anno Domini one thousand seven hundred and sixty one, Before his Majesty's Justices of the Peace for said County, to wit;

JAMES HAMILTON	NICHOLAS MINOR	&
AENEAS CAMPBELL	FRANCIS PEYTON	Gent.

     - JACOB FREDERICK CURTIUS, Plt. agt. JOHN MARTIN WINTNALE, Deft. In Debt

GEORGE FOUT of this County comes into Court and undertakes for Deft. that in case he shall be cast in this suit that he shall pay and satisfy the condemnation of the Court or render his body to Prison in execution for the same or that he, the said GEORGE FOUT, will do it for him. And Deft. in his proper person saving to himself all advantages of Exceptions as well to Plt.'s Writ as to his Declaration prays and has leave to imparl till next Court and then to plead

     - JOSEPH STEPHENS, an Evidence for JAMES LEITH against JAMES INGOE DOZER

p.   <u>Loudoun County Court 8th day of December 1761</u>
547   having attended Court two daies, ordered that JAMES LEITH pay him fifty pounds of tobacco for the same

     - WILLIAM DOUGLASS and ELIZABETH DOUGLASS his Wife, Plts. agt. EZEKIEL HICKMAN, Deft.   In Case

On motion of Plts. by their Attorney, a Commission is awarded them to examine and take the Depositions of their witnesses residing in the Province of MARYLAND giving Deft. legal notice of the time and place of executing the same, and the suit is continued till next Court

     - An Indenture of Feofment between WILLIAM THOMAS of one part and ROBERT SANDFORD of other part and Receipt and Memorandum of Livery of Seisin thereunder written were acknowledged by WILLIAM THOMAS and ordered to be recorded

     - An Indenture of Bargain and Sale between THOMAS CRITCHER and his Wife of the one part and JOHN EVINS of the other part and Receipt thereon endorsed were proved to be the act and deed of THOMAS CRITCHER by the Oath of JAMES COLEMAN and ARTHUR MORTIMORE, witnesses thereto

     - An Indenture of Feofment between JOHN CARGILL and CATHARINE his

Wife of one part and WILLIAM WEST, JUNR., of other part was acknowledged by
said JOHN and CATHARINE, she being first privily examined as the Law directs,
and the Memorandum of Livery of Seisin & Receipt thereon endorsed were acknowledged by said JOHN and together with the Indenture ordered to be recorded
    - Ordered that JAMES ROGERS be committed to the Stocks for a Misbe-
havior, there to remain for the space of four minutes
    - On motion of JOSEPH MORING, who is Comon Bail for JOHN McCARTY at
the suit of CRAVEN PEYTON, in two actions, and having proved that JOHN
McCARTY was taken out of his custody on the seventh day of this Instant by a
Warrant for Felony and carried for the Trial thereof into the County of PRINCE
WILLIAM, the same is ordered to be certified
    - JOHN HUTCHISON, GEORGE HEADEN, VINCENT LEWIS, JOHN
MOSS and PHILIP NOLAND who were ordered to be Fined at the last Court for not
appearing as Grand Jurors are for certain reasons appearing to this Court excused
    - Ordered that the Court be adjourned till tomorrow morning eight o'clock
    - The Minutes of these Proceedings were signed
                            " JAS: HAMILTON "

p.   - At a Court continued and held for Loudoun County at the Courthouse on
548   Wednesday the Ninth day of December one thousand seven hundred and sixty
one Before his Majesty's Justices of the Peace for the said County, to wit,
        JAMES HAMILTON   NICHOLAS MINOR   &
        AENEAS CAMPBELL   JOSIAS CLAPHAM   Gent.

    - The Petition of Messrs. JOSEPH WATSON and JOHN KIRKPATRICK
against SAMUEL COMPTON is dismissed, being agreed by the parties
    - JOHN WORMSLEY, Plt. agt. JOHN McCARTY, Deft.
  Upon an Attachment
This suit is dismissed being agreed by the parties
    - An Indenture of Feofment between NICHOLAS MINOR, Gent., of one part
and FLEMING PATTERSON of other part and Memorandum of Livery of Seisin
thereon endorsed, was acknowledged by NICHOLAS MINOR and ordered to be
recorded
    - An Indenture of Feofment between JOHN NEWTON, Gent., and BETTY his
Wife of one part and WILLIAM CARR LANE of other part and Memorandum of
Livery of Seisin and Receipt thereon endorsed, also a Bond for performance of Covenants, from JOHN NEWTON to WILLIAM CARR LANE were proved by the Oath of
JAMES LANE, Gent., witness thereto
    - Present.   JAMES LANE, Gent.
    - An Indenture of Feofment between NICHOLAS MINOR, Gent., of one part
and FLEMING PATTERSON of other part and Memorandum of Livery of Seisin
thereon endorsed were acknowledged by NICHOLAS MINOR and ordered to be
recorded
    - Absent. JOSIAS CLAPHAM, Gent.
    - WILLIAM GOSSETT, JUNR., Plt. agt. SAMUEL DAVIS, JUNR. Deft.
  In Trespass Assault and Battery
The Deft. being again returned not to be ound, on motion of Plt.'s Attorney another

Plurius Capias is awarded him returnable here at next Court
    - CRAVEN PEYTON, Plt. agt. JOHN PHILLIPS, Deft.   In Case
The Deft. being returned not to be found, on motion of Plt.'s Attorney an

p.   Loudoun County Court 9th of December 1761
549   Attachment is awarded him against Deft.'s Estate for fifteen pounds current
      money and costs returnable here at next Court
    - ANTHONY RUSSELL, Plt. agt. WILLIAM OWSLEY, Deft.   In Debt
The Deft. being arrested and not appearing altho' solemnly called, on moiton of Plt.
by FRANCIS DADE, his Attorney, it is ordered that unless Deft. shall appear here at
next Court and answer Plt.'s action, Judgment shall then be given for Plt. against him
and WILLIAM PEARLL who is returned Security for his appearance, for the Debt in
the Declaration mentioned and costs
    - LEE MASSEY, WILLIAM JETT, JUNR., CRAVEN PEYTON, JOHN
MOSS, JUNR. and PHILIP NOLAND, Gent., are by the Court recommended to the
Honorable FRANCIS FAUQUIER, Esqr., as proper persons to be added to the
Commission of the Peace for this County
    - WILLIAM McMANAMY and REBECCA his Wife, Plts. agt.
      RANDAL McALLISTER, Deft.   In Case
The Deft being returned not to be found, on motion of Plts. by their Attorney, an
Alias Capias is awarded them returnable here at next Court
    - WILLIAM BAKER, Plt. agt. JOHN DAVIS, Deft.   In Case
This day came the parties by their Attornies and Deft. saving to himself all advan-
tages of Exceptions as well to Plt.'s Writ as to his Declaration, prays and has leave to
imparl till next Court and then to plead
    - The Right Honble. CHARLES EARL of TANKERVILLE, Plt. agt.
      JOHN HOUGH, Deft.   In Trespass
This day came the parties by their Attornies and Deft. saving to himself all advantages of Exceptions as well to Plt.'s Writ as to his Declaration, prays and has leave to
imparl till next Court and then to plead
    - JOHN CARGILL, Plt. agt. FRANCIS BALLENGER, Deft.
      In Trespass Assault and Battery
Discontinued, the Plt. not further prosecuting
    - PATRICK CAIN, Plt. agt. JOHN MORRIS, Deft.
      In Trespass Assault and Battery
This suit is dismissed being agreed by the parties

p.   Loudoun County Court 9th of December 1761
550   - ARCHIBALD HENDERSON, Plt. agt. JOHN CAMDEN, Deft. In Debt
    The Defendant being arrested and not appearing altho' solemnly called, on
motion of Plt. by WILLIAM ELLZEY his Attorney, it is ordered that unless Deft. shall
appear here at next Court and answer Plt.'s action, Judgment shall then be given for
Plt. against him and JOHN CARGILL, who is returned Security for his appearance,
for the Debt in the Declaration mentioned and costs
    - SAMUEL PATTERSON, Plt. agt. PATRICK McKINZEY, Deft.   In Case
This day came the parties by their Attornies and Deft. saving to himself all advantages of Exceptions as well to Plt.'s Writ as to his Declaration, prays and has leave to

imparl till next Court and then to plead

    - ANDREW ADAM, Plt. agt. THOMAS AWBREY, Deft.   In Case

The Deft. being ruled to give Special Bail and failing so to do, on motion of Plt. by HUGH WEST, his Attorney, it is ordered that Judgment be entered for Plt. against Deft. and WILLIAM TRAMELL, his Security for the appearance of Deft. for what damages Plt. hath sustained by occasion of Deft.'s Breach of the Assumption in the Declaration specified, which damages are to be inquired of by a Jury unless Deft. find such Bail at the next Court and plead to issue

    - FRANCIS HERONIMUS, Plt. agt. WILLIAM RUST, Deft. In Trespass

The Deft. being returned not to be found, on motion of Plt.'s Attorney an Alias Capias is awarded him returnable here at next Court

    - ELIJAH CHINN, Plt. agt. BENJAMIN GRAYSON, Deft.   In Case

This day came the parties by their Attornies and Deft. saving to himself all advantages of Exceptions as well to Plt.'s Writ as to his Declaration, prays and has leave to imparl till next Court and then to plead

    - FLEMING PATTERSON, Plt. agt. JOHN WALMSLEY, Deft.

Discontinued, Plt. not further prosecuting

p. 551   Loudoun County Court 9th of December 1761

    - HENRY WISHEART, OWEN ROBERTS, FRANCIS SUMMERS, ELIJAH CHINN and HENRY MOORE who were ordered to be Fined at last Court for not appearing as Grand Jurors are for certain reasons appearing to the Court excused

    - The Petition of MARTIN ARMSTRONG against JERRY THOMAS is dismissed, being agreed by the parties

    - Ordered that OWEN ROBERTS be appointed Surveyor of the Road in the room of JAMES HAMILTON, Gent., who is discharged from that Office

    - Ordered that JAMES HAMILTON, Gent., allot the hands to work on the Roads whereof OWEN ROBERTS and JOHN HOUGH are Surveyors

    - NICHOLAS MINOR, Plt. agt. HENRY PEYTON, Deft.   In Debt

This day came as well Plt. by his Attorney as Deft. in his proper person and Deft. acknowledged Plt.'s action. Therefore it is considered by the Court that Plt. recover against Deft. one hundred seventy pounds, seventeen shillings and six pence, the Dect in the Declaration mentioned, and his costs by him about his suit in this behalf expended; and Deft. in mercy, &c., But this Judgment is to be discharged by paiment of eighty five pounds, eight shillings and nine pence together with Interest thereon to be computed after the rate of five percentum per annum from the twenty fifth day of July 1761 to the time of paiment and the costs. And Plt. agrees to stay execution of this Judgment till the last day of May next.

    - Ordered that the Court be adjourned till the second Tuesday in January next

    - The Minutes of these Proceedings were signed

                            " JAS: HAMILTON "

p. 552   - At a Court held for Loudoun County at the Courthouse on Tuesday the Ninth day of February in the second year of the Reign of our Sovereign Lord George the Third by the grace of God of Great Britain France and Ireland, King, Defender of the faith, &c. Anno Domini one thousand seven hundred and sixty two, Before his Majesty's Justices of the Peace for said County, to wit;

JAMES HAMILTON	RICHARD COLEMAN
NICHOLAS MINOR	FRANCIS PEYTON &
BENJAMIN GRAYSON	Gent.

    - A Commission for the acknowledgment and privy Examination of JANE HAGUE to Deeds of Lease and Release made between FRANCIS HAGUE and said JANE his Wife of one part and AENEAS CAMPBELL, Gent., of other part, for six hundred ninety two acres of land, and the Certificate of the Execution thereof was returned into Court and ordered to be recorded

    - A Commission for the acknowledgment and privy Examination of JANE HAGUE, to Deeds of Lease and Release made between FRANCIS HAGUE and said JANE his Wife of one part and AENEAS CAMPBELL, Gent. of other part for seventy one acres of land and the Certificate of Execution thereof was returned into Court and ordered to be recorded

    - Indentures of Lease and Release between RICHARD ROBERTS and ANN his Wife of one part and WILLIAM JONES of other part and Receipt thereon endorsed were acknowledged by said RICHARD and the Release was acknowledged by said ANN, she being first privily examined as the Law directs, and together with the Lease and Receipt ordered to be recorded

    - Indentures of Lease and Release between JOSEPH ROBERTS and AGNES his Wife of one part and JAMES STEER of other part and Receipt thereon endorsed were acknowledged by said JOSEPH and said Release was acknowledged by said AGNES, she having been first privily examined as the Law directs, and together with the Lease and Receipt ordered to be recorded

    - Ordered that WILLIAM BARKLEY be appointed Surveyor of the Road in the room of THOMAS WILLIAMS, who is discharged from that Office

    - WILLIAM WEST, Gent., Sherif of this County, with HUGH WEST, Gent., his Security, entered iinto and acknowledged Bond for collecting the County Levy laid and assessed in November last past which is ordered to be recorded

p.   <u>Loudoun County Court 9th of February 1762</u>

553   - JAMES VESSELL who stands bound by Recognizance to appear here this day to answer the Complaint of ROBERT HAMILTON against him for Breach of the Peace, appeared accordingly. Whereupon ROBERT HAMILTON and JAMES VESSEL were fully heard and ROBERT HAMILTON making Oath according to Law and requiring Security of the Peace against him, On consideration whereof, it is ordered that JAMES VESSELL be committed to the custody of the Sherif of this County there to remain untill he shall give Security for his good behavior for the space of one year from this time, and thereupon JAMES VESSELL with THOMAS LEWIS and WILLIAM ROSS, both of this County, came into Curt and acknowledged themselves severally indebted unto our Sovereign Lord George the Third King of Great Britain, &c., in the sums following, that is to say, JAMES VESSELL in the sum of twenty pounds and THOMAS LEWIS and WILLIAM ROSS in the sum of ten pounds of their respective lands and tenements goods and chattels to be levied and to our Lord the King his heirs and successors rendered, Yet upon this Condition, that if JAMES VESSELL shall be of good behavior towards all his Majesty's liege people and

more especially towards ROBERT HAMILTON for the space of one year from this time, Then the Recognizance to be void

    - Indentures of Lease and Release between AENEAS CAMPBELL, Gent., and LYDIA his Wife of one part and CHARLES BINNS, Gent., of other part and Receipt thereon endorsed, also a Bond from AENEAS CAMPBELL to CHARLES BINNS were acknowledged by AENEAS CAMPBELL and the Release was acknowledged by said LYDIA, she having been privily examinated as the Law directs, and together with the Lease, Receipt and Bond ordered to be recorded

    - An Indenture of Feofment between THOMAS PRITCHARD and RACHEL his Wife of one part and JACOB SHILLINGS of other part and Memorandum of Livery of Seisin thereon endorsed were acknowledged by said THOMAS and ordered to be recorded

    - Present AENEAS CAMPBELL, Gent.

    - On motion of JOHN HOUGH, it is ordered that the Report of the Jury for the valuation of an acre of land belonging to (blank) on GOOSE CREEK and the Order for vesting the same in JOHN HOUGH be set aside, And on Petition of said JOHN for leave to erect a Griss Mill over GOOSE CREEK and to have one acre of land belonging to the Children of SAMUEL SELDEN, Gent., on or near the Ford of said Creek, leading from LEESBURG to ALEXANDRIA, it is ordered that the Sherif summon a Jury of twelve Freeholders of the Vicinage to meet upon the land petitioned for, who being met and duly sworn before a Magistrate or the Sherif, shall diligently view and examained the land and the lands adjacent thereto on both sides the Run which may be affected or laid under water by building the Mill together with the Timber and other conveniences thereon and report the same with the value of the acre petitioned for and of the damages to the party holding the same or to any other person or persons under their hands and seals to the Court

    - On motion of JOHN CARLYLE, Gent., and JOHN HOUGH, it is ordered that they have leave to keep a Ferry from the Lower side of GOOSE CREEK in this County to the usual place of landing on the upper side

p.   <u>Loudoun County Court 9th of February 1762</u>
554   of said Creek in the Road leading from LEESBURG to ALEXANDRIA, it being the land formerly belonging to ANN MASON, Widow, and now said to be the land of the Children of SAMUEL SELDEN, Gent.

    - Ordered that a Licence be granted unto JOHN CARLYLE, Gent. and JOHN HOUGH to keep an ORDINARY on the lower side of GOOSE CREEK at the Ferry for one year, they with HUGH WEST, their Security, having entered into Bond as the Law directs

    - Ordered that the Churchwardens of Cameron Parish bind out JOHN PROCTER, a Mulatto base born Child to THOMAS KELLY according to Law

    - Ordered that a Licence be granted unto RICHARD COLEMAN, Gent., to keep ORDINARY at his House for one year, he with HUGH WEST, his Security, entered into Bond as the Law directs

    - Upon Petition of NICHOLAS MINOR, Gent., late Sherif of Loudoun County, against ROBERT WOOD for a Debt due by Account, This day came the parties by their Attornies and Deft. acknowledged Plt.'s demand for one pound, fifteen shillings and ten pence one penny to be just. Therefore it is considered by the Court that Plt.

recover against Deft. one pound, fifteen shillings and ten pence half penny and his costs by him in this behalf expended

 - Ordered that the Surveyor of the Road from LEESBRUG to GOOSE CREEK clear the Road to the usual Ferry Landing at the mouth of TUSCORORA

 - A Report of the persons appointed to view the most convenient way for a Road from THOMAS STUMP's Landing to LEESBURG was returned in these words, vist., "We the within nominated have agreable to the within Order viewed the most convenient Road and have markt it agreably, the said Road leads through Colo. FAIRFAX's Land as we believe, SAMUEL SMITH, WILLIAM SMITH, THOMAS STUMP." Whereupon it is ordered by the Court that the Road be cleared according to Law, that WILLIAM SMITH be appointed Surveyor thereof, and that JOHN MUCKLEHANEY, Gent., allot the hands to work thereon

 - Ordered that the Court be adjourned till tomorrow morning eight o'clock

 - The Minutes of these Proceedings were signed
" JAS: HAMILTON"

p. 555 - <u>At a Court continued and held for Loudoun County at the Courthouse on</u> Wednesday the Tenth day of February one thousand seven hundred and sixty two, Before his Majesty's Justices of the Peace for said County, to wit;

AENEAS CAMPBELL	RICHARD COLEMAN &
NICHOLAS MINOR	FRANCIS PEYTON, Gent.

 - THOMAS MIDDLETON, Plt. agt. JOHN WINN, Deft.   In Debt
This day came as well the Plt. by FRANCIS DADE, his Attorney, as Deft. in his proper person and Deft. relinquishing his former Plea saith that he cannot gainsay Plt.'s action; Therefore it is considered by the Court that Plt. recover against Deft. five pounds, eleven shillings and eight pence, the Debt in the Declaration mentioned, and his costs by him about his suit in this behalf expended, and Deft. in mercy, &c.

 - Upon Petition of MINOR WINN against JOHN OWSLEY for a Debt due by Account, This day came the parties in their proper persons and Deft. acknowledged Plt.'s demand for two pounds, two shillings and six pence to be just. Therefore it is considered by the Court that Plt. recover against Deft. the two pounds, two shillings and six pence and his costs by him in this behalf expended

 - Upon Petition of WILLIAM WINN against JOHN OWSLEY for a Debt due by Account, This day came the parties in their proper persons and Deft. acknowledged Plt.'s demand for three pounds, four shillings Virginia Currency to be just; Therefore it is considered by the Court that Plt. recover against Deft. the three pounds, four shillings and his costs by him in this behalf expended

 - Ordered that ISAAC FOUCH be appointed Surveyor of the Road in the room of WILLIAM ROSS, who is discharged from that Office

 - On Petition of HOLLAND MIDDLETON against JOHN PHILLIPS for a Debt due by Note of Hand, This day came Plt. by HUGH WEST, his Attorney, and Deft. having been duly served with a copy of the Petition and Summons was solemnly called but came not. Therefore it is considered by the Court that Plt. recover against Deft. three pounds and his costs in this behalf expended

 - On Petition of RICHARD BARTLESON against EDWARD HARDIN for a Debt due by Note of Hand, This day came as well Plt. by BENJAMIN SEBASTIAN his Attorney as Deft. in his proper person, and Deft acknowlefdged Plt.'s damand for four pounds, eleven shillings and two pence current money to be just. Therefore it is considered by the Court that Plt. recover against Deft.said four pounds eleven shillings and two pence

    - The Petition of CHRISTIAN PINKSTEAD against RICHARD KEEN is discontinued

p.   <u>Loudoun County Court 10th of February 1762</u>
556   - Upon Petition of RICHARD BARTLESON against MICHAEL VAN BUS-
KARCH for a Debt due by Note of Hand, This day came Plt. by BENJAMIN SEBASTIAN, his Attorney, and Deft. in his proper person and Deft. acknowledged Plt.'s demand for four pounds, twelve shillings and six pence current money of Virginia to be just; Therefore it is considered by the Court that Plt. recover against Deft. the four pounds, twelve shillings and six pence and his costs by him in this behalf expended

    - Upon Petition of RICHARD BARTLESON against ANTHONY PARKER and CHARLES SWAIN for a Debt due by Account, This day came Plt. by BENJA-MIN SEBASTIAN, his Attorney, and Defts. having been duly summoned were solemnly called but came not. Therefore it is considered by the Court that Plt. recover against Defts. two pounds, fifteen shillings and his costs by him in this behalf expended

    - Upon Petition of RICHARD BARTLESON against JOHN GOLLOWAY for a Debt due by Account, This day came Plt. by BENJAMIN SEBASTIAN, his Attor-ney, and Deft. having been duly summoned was solemnly called but came not. There-fore it is considered by the Court tha Plt. recover against Deft. two pounds, six shillings and six pence and his costs by him in this behalf expended

    - An Indenture of Feofment between NICHOLAS MINOR of one part and THOMAS PRITCHARD of other part and Memorandum of Livery of Seisin thereon endorsed were acknowledged by said NICHOLAS and ordered to be recorded

    - Present. JAMES HAMILTON & JOSIAS CLAPHAM, Gent.

    - Upon Petition of EDWARD SNIGGERS against GRIFITH MATTHIAS for a Debt due by Note of Hand, This day came Plt. by HUGH WEST, his Attorney, and Deft. having been duly summoned was solemnly called but came not; Therefore it is considered by the Court that Plt. recover against Deft. two pounds, fifteen shillings and his costs by him in this behalf expended, including seven shillings and six pence for a Lawyer's fee

    - SAMUEL DAVIS, JUNR., JOHN DAVIS, WILLIAM FURR and WILLIAM ALLAN wre brought before the Court in custody of WILLIAM WEST, Gent., Sherif of this County, for behaving in a riotous manner in breaking his Majesty's Peace in the presence of FRANCIS PEYTON, Gent., one of his Majesty's Justices of the Peace for this County, on the Ninth day of this Instant in the night time, and thereupon

WILLIAM BAKER	WILLIAM WINN	ARCHIBALD CRAWFORD
MARTIN ARMSTRONG	WILLIAM WEST	CRAVEN PEYTON
CATHARINE DODD,	WILLIAM DODD and	JOHN WINN

were sworn and examined as witnesses against said SAMUEL DAVIS, JUNR., JOHN DAVIS, WILLIAM FURR and WILLIAM ALLAN and they heard in their defence. On consideration whereof, it is ordered that they remain in custody of the

Sherif till they give security for their personal appearance here on the second Tuesday in May next then and there to answer the same before the Grand Jury to be then impannelled and sworn

p. 557 Loudoun County Court 10th of February 1762

and thereupon said SAMUEL DAVIS with THOMAS OWSLEY, JOHN OWSLEY and EDWARD GARRETT, his Securities, in open Court acknowledged themselves indebted to our Sovereign Lord King George the Third his heirs and successors, that is to say, SAMUEL DAVIS in the sum of Fifty pounds and THOMAS OWSLEY, JOHN OWSLEY and EDWARD GARRETT in sum of twenty five pounds each to be levied of their respective goods and chattels lands and tenements and to our said Lord the King his heirs and successors rendered, Yet on the Condition that if said SAMUEL DAVIS shall make his personal appearance here on the second Tuesday in May next, then and thereto answer the Indictment to be exhibited against him for a Riot and such other things as shall be then and there objected against him on his Majesty's behalf and in the mean time to be of good behavior towards all his Majesty's liege people and not to depart thence without leave of the Court, Then this Recognizance to be void, else to remain in full force

- JOHN DAVIS with THOMAS OWSLEY, JOHN OWSLEY and EDWARD GARRETT, his Securities, in open Court severally acknowledged themselves indebted to our Sovereign Lord George the Third his heirs and successors, that is to say, JOHN DAVIS in the sum of fifty pounds and THOMAS OWSLEY, JOHN OWSLEY and EDWARD GARRETT in the sum of twenty five pounds each to be levied of their respective goods and chattels, lands and tenements and to our Lord the King his heirs and successors rendered, Yet upon condition that if JOHN DAVIS shall make his personal appearance here on the second Tuesday in May next then and there to answer an Indictment to be exhibited against him for a Riot and such other things as shall be then and there objected to against him on his Majesty's behalf and in the mean time to be of good behavior towards all his Majesty's liege people and not to depart thence without leave of the Court, then this Recognizance to be void or else to remain in full force

- WILLIAM FURR with THOMAS OWSLEY, JOHN OWSLEY and EDWARD GARRETT, his Securities, severlly acknowledged themselves indebted to our Sovereign Lord George the Third his heirs and successors, that is to say, WILLIAM FURR in the sum of fifty pounds and THOMAS OWSLEY, JOHN OWSLEY and EDWARD GARRETT in the sum of twenty five pounds each to be levied of their goods and chattels, lands and tenements and to our Lord the King his heirs and successors rendered, Yet upon condition that if WILLIAM FURR shall make his personal appearance here on the second Tuesday in May next then and there to answer an Indictment to be exhibited against him for a Riot and such other things as shall be then and there objected to against him on his Majesty's behalf and in the mean time to be of good behavior towards all his Majesty's liege people and not to depart thence without leave of the Court, then this Recognizance to be void or else to remain in full force

- WILLIAM ALLAN with THOMAS OWSLEY, JOHN OWSLEY and EDWARD GARRETT, his Securities, in open Court acknowledged themselve indebted unto our Sovereign Lord King George

p.   Loudoun County Court 10th of February 1762
558   the Third his heirs and successors, that is to say, WILLIAM ALLAN in sum
       of fifty pounds and THOMAS OWSLEY, JOHN OWSLEY and EDWARD
GARRETT in sum of twenty five pounds to be levied of their respective goods and
chattels lands and tenements and to our Lord the King his heirs and successors rendered, Yet upon condition that if WILLIAM ALLAN shall make his personal appearance here on the second Tuesday in May next then and there to answer an Indictment to be exhibited against him for a Riot and such other things as shall be then and
there objected against him on his Majesty's behalf and in the mean time to be of good
behavior towards all his Majesty's liege people and not to depart thence without leave
of the Court, Then this Recognizance to be void else to remain in full force
       - The Petition of WILLIAM DODD against JAMES VESSELLS is continued
till next Court at motion and costs of Deft.
       - The Petition of THOMAS PHILLIPS against JOSIAS CLAPHAM, Gent., is
continued till next Court at motion and costs of Plt.
       - The Petition of JACOB GARDNER against SAMUEL WINN is continued
till next Court at motion and costs of Plt.
       - Upon Petition of BENJAMIN GRAYSON and CRAVEN PEYTON against
PETER WILLSON for a Debt due by Bill. This day came Plts. by HUGH WEST,
their Attorney, and Deft. having been duly summoned was solemnly called but came
not; Therefore it is considered by the Court that Plts. recover against Deft. one
pound, nineteen shillings and three pence with lawful Interest thereon from the first
day of September 1760 till paiment and their costs by them in this behalf expended,
including seven shillings and six pence for a Lawyer's fee
       - The Petition of JOHN MEHERG against WILLIAM HUTCHISON is con-
tinued till next Court by consent of the parties
       - Upon Petition of AENEAS CAMPBELL, Gent., against JOHN KELLIHAM
for a Debt due by Account, This day came as well Plt. by HUGH WEST, his Attorney
as Deft. in his proper person who being fully heard, it is considered by the Court that
Plt. recover against Deft. six shillings and one penny half penny and his costs by him
in this behalf expended
       - Upon Petition of AENEAS CAMPBELL, Gent. against JEREMIAH THO-
MAS for a Debt due by Account; This day came Plt. by HUGH WEST, his Attorney,
and Deft. having been duly summoned was solemnly called but came not; Therefore it
is considered by the Court that Plt. recover against Deft. one pound, eighteen shillings
and six pence and his costs by him in this behalf expended

p.   Loudoun County Court 10th of February 1762
559   - Upon Petition of CRAVEN PEYTON against THOMAS AWBREY for a
       Debt due by Account, This day came Plt. by HUGH WEST, his Attorney, and
Deft. having been duly summoned was solemnly called but came not; Therefore it is
considered by the Court that Plt. recover against Deft. five pounds and his costs by
him in this behalf expended
       - The Petition of SETH JOHNSON against THOMAS TRAMMELL is con-
tinued till next Court at motion and costs of Deft.
       - The Petition of WILLIAM DODD against JAMES GOULDING is continued
till next Court at motion and costs of Deft.

- The Petition of STIRMAN CHILTON against THOMAS PRITCHARD is continued till next Court at motion and costs of Deft.
- The Petition of WILLIAM OWSLEY against WILLIAM BURKLEY is continued till next Court by consent of the parties
- ThePetition of FRANCIS HERONIMOUS against JOHN WALDEN is continued till next Court by consent of the parties
- The Petition of JOHN OWSLEY against WILLIAM CONNELL is continued till next Court at motion and costs of Deft.
- The Petition of JAMES HOOK against THOMAS MIDDLETON is continued till next Court by consent of the parties
- ThePetition of JAMES FOWLER against PHILIP FOUGHT is discontinued
- ThePetition of ANTHONY RUSSELL, Gent., against JAMES DONELSON is discontinued
- The Petition of JOHN POSEY against WILLIAM OWSLEY is continued till next Court at motion and costs of Deft.
- Upon Petition of ANTHONY RUSSELL, Gent., against JAMES DONELSON for a Debt due by Account, This day came Plt. by FRANCIS DADE his Attorney and Deft. having been duly summoned was solemnly called but came not; Therefore it is considered by the Court that Plt. recover against Deft. two pounds, twelve shlllings and ten pence and his costs by him in this behalf expended
- ThePetition of JOSEPH STEPHENS against JOSEPH JANNEY is continued till next Court at motion and costs of Deft.
- The Petition of WILLIAM ELLZEY against HENRY PARKER is continued till next Court by consent of the parties
- Upon Petition of DAVID SMITH against FRANCIS ROSE for a Debt due by Note of Hand, This day came Plt. in his proper person and Deft. having been duly summoned was solemnly called but came not; Therefore it is considered by the Court that Plt. recover against Deft. two hundred pounds of crop tobacco and his costs by him in this behalf expended

p. 560   Loudoun County Court 10th of February 1762
- Upon Petition of DENNIS DALLIS against JOHN PYLES for a Debt due by Account, This day came the parties by their Attornies, who being fully heard, it is considered by the Court that Plt. recover against Deft. one pound, seventeen shillings and five pence farthing and his costs by him in this behalf expended
- The Petition of DENNIS DALLIS against JONATHAN DAVIS is continued till next Court at motion and costs of Plt.
- Upon Petition of CRAVEN PEYTON against JOHN GOLLOWAY for a Debt due by Account; This day came Plt. by HUGH WEST, his Attorney, and Deft. having been dully served with a copy of the Petition and Summons was duly called but came not; Therefore it is considered by the Court that Plt. recover against Deft. two pounds ten shillings and two pence and his costs by him in this behalf expended
- Upon Petition of CRAVEN PEYTON against TARVIN ARTIST for a Debt due by Account, This day came Plt. by HUGH WEST, his Attorney, and Deft. having been duly served with a Copy of the Petition and Summons was solemnly called but came not; Therefore it is considered by the Court that Plt. recover against Deft. four pounds and his costs by him in this behalf expended

- The Petition of JACOB SHILLING against JAMES VESSELLS is continued till next Court at motion and costs of Deft.

- CRAVEN PEYTON, Plt. agt. JOHN OWSLEY, otherwise called I JOHN OWSLEY of Loudoun County, Planter, Deft.   In Debt

This day came as well Plt. by HUGH WEST, his Attorney, and Deft. in his proper person and Deft. acknowledged Plt.'s action. Therefore it is considered by the Court that Plt. recover against Deft. seventy pounds, fourteen shillings and one penny current money, the Debt in the Declaration mentioned, and his costs by him about his suit in this behalf expended; And Deft. in mercy, &c., But this Judgment is to be discharged by paiment of twenty one pounds and four pence half penny current money with Interest for the same to be computed after the rate of five percentum per annum from the first day of March 1760 till paiment and the costs

- Ordered that the Court be adjourned till the second Tuesday in March next
- The Minutes of these Proceedings were signed
                    " JAS: HAMILTON "

p.   - At a Court held for Loudoun County at the Courthouse on Tuesday the
561   Ninth day of March in the second year of the Reign of our Sovereign Lord
      George the Third by the grace of God of Great Britain, France and Ireland,
King, Defender of the faith,&c., Anno Domini one thousand seven hundred and sixty two, Before his Majesty's Justices of the Peace for the said County, to wit;

JAMES HAMILTON   FRANCIS PEYTON   &
NICHOLAS MINOR   JOHN MUCKLEHANEY,   Gent.

- Indentures of Lease and Release between MICHAEL GREGG and SARAH his Wife of one part and ISAAC NICHOLS of other part and Receipt thereon endorsed were proved by the Affirmation of THOMAS GREGG, WILLIAM TATE and JAMES PHILLIPS (Quakers) witnesses thereto, and ordered to be recorded

- Indentures of Lease and Release between THOMAS PHILLIPS and JEAN his Wife of one part and ALEXANDER ARNETT of the other part and the Receipt thereon endorsed were acknowledged by said THOMAS and JEAN, she having been first privily examined as the Law directs, and ordered to be recorded

- The Inventory and Appraisment of the Estate of JOSEPH McGEACH, deced., was returned and is ordered to be recorded

            - Present   JOSIAS CLAPHAM, Gent.

- An Indenture of Feoffment between JOSEPH SCRIEVE of one part and JACOB READ of other part and Memorandum of Livery of Seisin and Receipt thereon endorsed were acknowledged by said JOSEPH and ordered to be recorded

            - Present. NICHOLAS MINOR, Gent.

- On motion of SARAH GEORGE, who made Oath according to Law, and together with THOMAS LEWIS and MARK CHILTON, her Securities, entered into and acknowledged Bond; Certificate is granted her for obtaining Letters of Administration on the Estate of TRAVERS GEORGE, deced., in due form

- Ordered that WILLIAM SMITH, THOMAS SHORES, WILLIAM MUSGROVE and NOTLEY WILLIAMS or any three thereof being first sworn before a Justice of this County, do appraise in current money the slaves (if any) and personal Estate of TRAVERS GEORGE, deced., in th said County and return the Appraisment to the Court

- Ordered that GILBERT SIMPSON, SAMPSON DORRELL, THOMAS SMITH and EDWARD WILLIAMS or any three thereof being first sworn before a Justice of FAIRFAX County, do appraise in current money the slaves (if any) and personal Estate of TRAVERS GEORGE, deced., in that Court, and return the Appraisment to the Court

- Ordered that the Sherif summon twenty four of the most capable Freeholders of this County to meet here on the second Tuesday in May next to serve as a Grand Jury of Inquest for the body of this County

- The Inventory and Appraisment of the Estate of JAMES SPURR, deced., was returned into Court and ordered to be recorded

- An Indenture of Feofment between JACOB REED of one part and ISAAC AUSTINN of other part and Receipt and Memorandum of Livery of Seisin thereon endorsed were acknowledged by said JACOB and ordered to be recorded

- Present. NICHOLAS MINOR, Gent.

- IMMANUEL LAY, SYLVANUS LAY and SAMUEL JENKINS being recognized to appear here this day on Suspicion of Hog Stealing appeared according to their Recognizance and the Proceedings

p.   **Loudoun County Court 9th of March 1762**
562` appearing to the Court to be irregular, it is ordered that the same be dismissed

- Ordered that the Court be adjourned till tomorrow morning eight o'clock
- The Minutes of these Proceedings were signed

" JAS: HAMILTON "

- At a Court continued and held for Loudoun County at the Courthouse on Wednesday the Tenth day of March one thousand seven hundred and sixty two Before his Majesty's Justices of the Peace for the said County, to wit;

| NICHOLAS MINOR | FRANCIS PEYTON | & |
| RICHARD COLEMAN | JOHN MUCKLEHANEY | Gent. |

- The Court proceeded to Rate the Liquors for this County as follows, vizt.

	S. D.
For a Gallon of Rum and so in proportion	10/
Nantz Brandy	10/
Peach and Apple Brandy	6/
New England Rum	2/6
Virginia Brandy from Grain	5/
Arack the Quart made into Punch	10/
A Quart of white, red or Madeira Wines	3/6
Foyall and other low Wines	1/6
English Strong Beer the Quart bottle	1/3
London Beer called Porter the Quart	1/
Virginia Strong Beer the Quart	/6
Cyder the Quart	/4
English Cyder the Quart bottle	1/3
A Gill of Rum made into Punch	/7 1/2
ditto with Fruit	/9
ditto without Fruit and made with Brown Sugar	/6

A good hot Diet without Beer or Cyder	/10
A Cold ditto	/6
A Gallon of Corn or Oats	/6
Stableage and Fodder for a Horse 24 hours or one night	/7 1/2
Pasturage for ditto 24 hours or one night	/4
Lodging in clean Sheets one night 6d., otherwise nothing	

p.   Loudoun County Court 10th of March 1762
563   - Ordered that the several and respective ORDINARY KEEPERS in this
        County do sell according to the above Rates in money or tobacco at the rate of
125 p ct. and that they do not presume to demand more of any person whatsoever
        - Indentures of Lease and Release between JOHN GLADIN and MARY his
Wife of one part and ROBERT ADAM of other part and Receipt thereon endorsed
were proved by the Oath of FLEMING PATTERSON, a witness thereto
        - NICHOLAS MINOR, Gent., acknowledged da counter part of an Indenture of
Apprenticeship for his Son, SPENCE MINOR, to ROBERT ADAM, Gent., which is
ordered to be certified
        - PATRICK O'CAIN being brought to the Court on Suspicion of his being
Guilty of Stealing on the last night, a Bridle and Saddle, the property of JOHN CAR-
GYLE, a Bridle the propert of JOHN SASSER and a Bridle the property of WIL-
LIAM BEAVIS, one Bell and Petticoat the property of JOHN DAVIS, by a Warrant
from JOSEPH CLAPHAM, Gent., one of his Majesty's Justices of the Peace for this
County, and said PATRICK being asked whether he was Guilty of the offence aforesaid or not, he confessed that he was thereof Guilty; and thereupon submitted himself
to the Judgment of the Court now sitting to inflict on him any Punishment that the
Justices should think proper. Therefore it is considered by the Justices that he
receive at the Public Whiping Post thirty lashes on his bare back well laid on and it is
commanded the Sherif that he cause immediate execution thereof to be done and
nothing further appearing against him, it is ordered that he be then discharged out of
custody
        - EDWARD NORTON, Plt. agt. WILLIAM CHILTON and WILLIAM
        SAUNDERS, Defts.   In Debt
This suit is dismissed, being agreed by the parties
        - JOHN HERYFORD, Plt. agt. RICHARD OSGOODTHARP Deft. In Case
This suit is dismissed, being agreed by the parties
        - THOMAS HARRISON, JAMES NISBET, BENJAMIN GRAYSON and
        SPENCE GRAYSON, Exrs. of the Last Will and Testament of BENJAMIN
        GRAYSON, Gent., deced., Plts. agt. THOMAS LEWELLING, Deft. In Case
This suit is dismissed, being agreed by the parties
        - JOHN DAVIS and MARGARET his Wife, Admrx. of THOMAS DAVIS,
        deced., Plts. against JOHN KING, Exr. of RICHARD OSBORN, deced., Deft.
        In Debt
On motion of Plts. by their Attorney, further time is allowed them to reply to the
Bill the next Court

p.   Loudoun County Court 10th of March 1762
564   - Upon the Petition of JOHN MUIR against WILLIAM DODD for a Debt due
        by Account. This day came Plt. by BENJAMIN SEBASTIAN, his Attorney,

and Deft. in his proper person and Deft. acknowledged Plt.'s demand for four pounds to be just. Therefore it is considered by the Court that Plt. recover against Deft. the four pounds and his costs by him in this behalf expended, including seven shillings and six pence for a Lawyer's fee

    - Indentures of Lease and Release between JOSEPH GARDNER and ROBERT WOOD of one part and JACOB REED of other part and Receipt thereon endorsed were proved by the Oaths of GILBERT SIMPSON, ROBERT STRETCH-BERRY and ISAAC SIMPSON WRIGHT, the witnesses thereto, and ordered to be recorded

    - HENRY PEYTON, Gent., Plt. agt. SAMUEL STILLWELL, Deft. In Case

    This day came the parties by their Attornies and thereupon came also a Jury to wit;

MICHAEL VAN BUSCARK	THOMAS PRITCHARD	STIRMAN CHILTON
JOHN CARGILE	THOMAS MIDDLETON	JAMES VESSELL
CHARLES CHILTON	ROBERT POPKINS	BENJAMIN SHREIVE
WILLIAM ROSS	JOHN LEWIS and	JOSEPH STEPHENS

who being elected tried and sworn the truth to speak upon the issue joined, upon their Oath do say that Deft. is Guilty in manner and form as Plt. against im hath declared and they do assess Plt.'s damages by occasion thereof to five pounds, ten shillings besides his costs. Therefore it is considered by the Court that Plt. recover against Deft. his damages aforesaid in form aforesaid assessed and his costs by him in this behalf expended, and Deft. in mercy, &c.

    - Ordered that a Licence be granted to MICAJAH POWELL to keep ORDINARY at LEESBURG for one year, he with CRAVEN PEYTON, his Security, having entered into Bond as the Law directs

    - JAMES WILLSON, Plt. agt. THOMAS RODGERS, Deft.

    Upon an Attachment

This day came Plt. by WILLIAM ELLZEY, his Attorney, and Deft. altho' solemnly called came not. Therefore it is considered by the Court that Plt. recover against Deft. four pounds, nineteen shillings and eleven pence and his costs by him in this behalf expended, and Deft. in mercy, &c.

It is ordered that the Sherif make sale of the goods delivered up to him by Garnishees, JOHN ANDERSON and VACHEL HOWARD according to L aw and out of the money arising from such sale pay and satisfy Plt.'s Debt and costs if they sell for so much and render the overplus, if any, to Deft.

    - Present.   JOSIAS CLAPHAM, Gent.

p.
565   Loudoun County Court 10th of March 1762

    - CRAVEN PEYTON, Plt. agt. JOHN McCARTY, Deft.

    Upon an Attachment

This suit is discontinued, the Plt. not further prosecuting

    - JOSEPH JANNEY, Plt. agt. JOHN McCARTY, Deft. Upon an Attachment Continued till next Court

    - JOHN DAVIS, Plt. agt. JOHN McCARTY, Deft. Upon an Attachment Continued till next Court

    - JAMES VESSELLS agt. JOHN McCARTY, Deft. Upon an Attachment Continued till next Court

    - ANDREW ADAM and FLEMING PATTERSON, Plts. agt.

JOHN McCARTY, Deft.   Upon an Attachment

Continued till next Court
    - BENJAMIN EDWARDS, Plt. agt. JOHN McCARTY, Deft.
    Upon an Attachment
Continued till next Court
    - AENEAS CAMPBELL, Plt. agt. HENRY PICKRELL, Deft.
    Upon an Attachment
This suit is dismissed being agreed by the parties
    - Messrs. ADAM and PATTERSON, Plts. agt. HENRY PICKRELL, Deft.
    Upon an Attachment
This suit is dismissed, being agreed by the parties
    - JOHN EVANS, Plt. agt. HENRY PICKRELL, Deft.   Upon an Attachment
This suit is dismissed, being agreed by the parties

p.
566
    <u>Loudoun County Court 10th of March 1762</u>
    - FLEMING PATTERSON, Plt. agt. GRIFFITH EVANS, Deft.
    Upon an Attachment
OWEN ROBERTS, a Garnishee, being sworn and declaring that he has nothing of
Deft.'s effects in his hands is discharged. JOHN HERYFORD being sworn declares
that he has in his hands of Deft.'s effects six shillings and ten pence. It is ordered that
he pay the same to Plt. JOHN EVANS being summoned as a Garnishee in this suit,
and failing to appear, an Attachment is awarded against him for his contempt returnable here at next Court; and the suit is continued
    - James a boy and Jenny a girl, Negroes belonging to PATRICK O'BRYON are
adjudged by the Court, James to be thirteen years and Jenny to fourteen years of age
    - JOHN DAVIS, Plt. agt. ALEXANDER BOWLIN, Deft.
    Upon an Attachment
This day came Plt. in his proper person and Deft. came not altho' solemnly called.
Therefore it is considered by the Court that Plt. recover against Deft. three pounds,
fifteen shillings and two hundred fifty pounds of tobacco and his costs by him in this
behalf expended and the Deft. in mercy, &c.
CHRISTOPHER PERFECT, a Constable for this County, having returned that he
had levied this Attachment on a black Gelding and some Hogs, it is ordered that he
sell the same according to Law and out of the money arising from such sale pay and
satisfy the Plt. his Debt and costs if they sell for so much and render the overplus if
any to the Deft.
    - WILLIAM DOUGLASS, Plt. agt. JOHN THOMAS alias JNO: TOMAS,
    Deft.   Upon an Attachment
This day came Plt. by HUGH WEST, his Attorney, and Deft. came not altho'
solemnly called. Therefore it is considered by the Court that Plt. recover against Deft.
three pounds, ten shillings and his costs by him in this behalf expended, and Deft. in
mercy, &c.
CHRISTOPHER PERFECT, a Garnishee, being sworn and declaring that he has
nothing of the Deft.'s effects in his hands is discharged. DANIEL JAMES being also
sworn declares

p.
567
    <u>Loudoun County Court 10th of March 1762</u>
    that he has in his hands of Deft.'s effects three pounds, five shillings and six

pence, it being the ballance due the Deft.'s Wife for one year's Wages. It is ordered that said DANIEL pay the same to Plt.

- The Petition of AENEAS CAMPBELL, Gent., against SHADRICK SHAVERS is discontinued

- The Petition of AENEAS CAMPBELL, Gent. against GEORGE GREGG is discontinued

- The Petition of AENEAS CAMPBELL, Gent. against JOHN BALL is discontinued

- The Petition of AENEAS CAMPBELL, Gent. against GEORGE NORMAN is dismissed, being agreed by the parties and it is ordered that Deft. pay unto Plt. his costs

- AENEAS CAMPBELL, Gent. agt. THOMAS JENKINS,   On Petition   The Deft. being returned not found, ordered that another Summons issue against him returnable here at next Court

- Upon Petition of AENEAS CAMPBELL, Gent., against JOHN WILKS for a Debt due by Account; This day came Plt. in his proper person and Deft. having been duly summoned was solemnly called but came not; Therefore it is considered by the Court that Plt. recover against Deft. two pounds, two shillings and eight pence half penny and his costs by him in this behalf expended

- Upon Petition of AENEAS CAMPBELL, Gent., against ROBERT STRETCHBERRY for a Debt due by Account, This day came Plt. in his proper person and Deft. having been duly summoned was solemnly called but came not. Therefore it is considered by the Court that Plt. recover against Deft. two pounds, seven shillings and his costs by him in this behalf expended

- LEVEN POWELL, an Evidence for HENRY PEYTON, Gent., against SAMUEL STILLWELL, having attended Court five daies and for travelling thirty miles from PRINCE WILLIAM County and returning three times, ordered that said HENRY pay him three hundred ninety four pounds of tobacco for the same

- WILLIAM SPEAKMAN, an Evidence for HENRY PEYTON, Gent., against SAMUEL STILLWELL, having attended Court six daies and for travelling thirty miles from PRINCE WILLIAM County and returning three times, ordered that said HENRY pay him four hundred twenty pounds of tobacco for the same

- JOHN CHAMP, an Evidence for HENRY PEYTON, Gent. against SAMUEL STILLWELL having attended Court five daies, ordered that said HENRY pay him one hundred twenty five pounds of tobacco for the same

- Ordered that the Churchwardens of Cameron Parish bind out JOHN RAWDERY, an Orphan, to JOHN TRAMMELL according to Law who is to learn him the Trade of a Cooper

p.   Loudoun County Court 10th of March 1762
568   - MINOR WINN, an Evidence for HENRY PEYTON, Gent., against SAMUEL STILLWELL, having attended Court six daies and for travelling sixteen miles from PRINCE WILLIAM County and returning four times, ordered that said HENRY pay him three hundred and forty two pounds of tobacco for the same

- On Petition of JOHN MOSS and HUGH WEST, Securities for MARY, the Wife of JONATHAN MONKHOUSE, her administration of the Estate of her late Husband, HENRY ANSLEY, deced., it is ordered that said JONATHAN and MARY be summoned to appear here at next Court to shew why they should not give other or counter security or deliver up the Estate to JOHN MOSS and HUGH WEST

- Present. CHARLES TYLER, Gent.

- Indentures of Lease and Release between WILLIAM ELLZEY and ALICE his Wife of one part and ANTHONY RUSSELL of other part and Receipt thereon endorsed were acknowledged by said WILLIAM and together with a Commission for taking the acknowledgment and privy examination of said ALICE and the Certificate of the execution thereof, ordered to be recorded

- AENEAS CAMPBELL, Gent. agt. ROBERT WOOD, Deft.   In Case

This day came as well Plt. by HUGH WEST, his Attorney, as Deft. in his proper person and Deft. acknowledged Plt.'s action for five pounds, two shillings and four pence. Therefore it is considered by the Court that Plt. recover against Deft. the five pounds, two shillings and four pence and his costs by him in this behalf expended and Deft. in mercy, &c.

- JAMES ROGERS, Plt. agt. JOHN HALL, Deft. In Trespass

This day came the parties by their Attornies and thereupon came also a Jury, to

wit | JOHN LEWIS | THOMAS CARTWRIGHT | ROBERT POPKINS |
EZEKIEL HICKMAN	THOMAS LEWIS	DAVID SMITH
JAMES VESSELL	MICHAEL VAN BUSCARK	STIRMAN CHILTON
JOHN CARGYLE	THOMAS MIDDLETON and	LEVEN POWELL

who being elected tried and sworn the truth to speak upon the issue joined, upon their Oath do say that Deft. is Not Guilty as in pleading he hath alledged. Therefore it is considered by the Court that Plt. take nothing by his Bill but for his false clamour be in mercy, &c., and Deft. go thereof without day and recover against Plt. his costs by him about his defence in this behalf expended

- Ordered that the Sherif summon THOMAS AWBREY to appear here at next Court to answer the Petition of JESSE HALL for ill usage and that the Sherif bring said JESSE before the Court at the same time

p.   Loudoun County Court 10th of March 1762
569   - JAMES ROGERS, Plt. agt. SAMUEL WINN Deft.   In Trespass

This day came the parties by their Attornies and thereupon came also a Jury

to wit | JOHN LEWIS | THOMAS CARTWRIGHT | ROBERT POPKINS |
EZEKIEL HICKMAN	THOMAS LEWIS	DAVID SMITH
JAMES VESSELL	MICHAEL VAN BUSCARK	STIRMAN CHILTON
JOHN CARGYLE	THOMAS MIDDLETON and	LEVEN POWELL

who being elected tried and sworn the truth to speak upon the issue joined, upon their Oath do say that Deft. is Not Guilty as in pleading he hath alledged. Therefore it is considered by the Court that Plt. take nothing by his Bill but for his false clamour be in mercy, &c., and Deft. go thereof without day and recover against Plt. his costs by him about his defence in this behalf expended

- ELIZABETH MORRIS, Wife of CHARLES MORRIS, an Evidence for SAMUEL WINN at the suit of JAMES ROGERS, having attended Court five daies, ordered that SAMUEL WINN pay said CHARLES one hundred twenty five pounds of tobacco for the same

- MARY MORRIS, the Wife of JOHN MORRIS, an Evidence of SAMUEL WINN at the suit of JAMES ROGERS, having attended Court five daies, ordered that SAMUEL WINN pay said JOHN one hundred twenty five pounds of tobacco for the same.

    - SUSANNA CAPES, an Evidence for SAMUEL WINN at the suit of JAMES ROGERS, having attended Court one day, ordered that said SAMUEL pay her twenty five pounds of tobacco for the same

    - JACOB GARDNER, an Evidence of JAMES ROGERS against SAMUEL WINN, having attended Court eleven daies, ordered that said JAMES pay him two hundred and seventy five pounds of tobacco for the same

    - BENJAMIN CHANDLER, an Evidence for JAMES ROGERS against SAMUEL WINN, having attended Court eleven daies and for travelling sixteen miles from PRINCE WILLIAM County and returning six times, ordered that said JAMES pay him five hundred sixty three pounds of tobacco for the same

    - The Right Honble. CHARLES EARL of TANKERVILLE, Plt. agt.
       JOHN HOUGH, Deft.   In Trespass

This day came the parties by their Attornies and Deft. saith that he is Not Guilty of the Trespass in manner and form as Plt. against him hath complained and of this he putteth himself upon the Country and Plt. likewise. And it being suggested by Plt.'s Attorney that the bounds of the Land are in question, it is ordered that the Surveyor of this County do go upon the Land where the Trespass is supposed to be committed on the (blank) day of (blank) next if fair, if not the next fair day and survey and lay off the Land in dispute, having regard to all Patents and Evidences that shall be produced by either of the parties and report all matters of Fact and Evidence specially to next Court and that

p.   <u>Loudoun County Court 10th of March 1762</u>
570   he return two fair Platts of the land to the Clerk's Office before the day of hearing and the Sheriff is to attend the Survey and remove force if any shall be offered

    - Ordered that the Court be adjourned till tomorrow morning eight o'clock
    - The Minutes of these Proceedings were signed
                " AENS. CAMPBELL "

    - At a Court continued and held for Loudoun County at the Courthouse on Thursday the Eleventh day of March one thousand seven hundred and sixty two, Before his Majesty's Justices of the Peace of the said County, to wit;

JAMES HAMILTON	CHARLES TYLER	
NICHOLAS MINOR	JOSIAS CLAPHAM	&
RICHARD COLEMAN	FRANCIS PEYTON	Gent.

    - The Petition of JAMES HOOK against THOMAS MIDDLETON is continued till next Court by consent of the parties

    - The Inventory and Appraisment of the Estate of GABRIEL ADAMS, deced., was returned and ordered to be recorded

    - JOHN DAVIS, Plt. agt. ELIZABETH LEWIS, Deft.   In Case

This day came the parties by their Attornies and thereupon came also a Jury, to wit

JOHN MUIR	BENJAMIN MASON	WILLIAM WINN
SAMUEL WINN	LEVEN POWELL	EZEKIEL HICKMAN
JOHN MINOR	MARK CHILTON	THOMAS MIDDLETON
MARTIN ARMSTRONG	CHARLES CHILTON and	MICHAEL VAN BUSCART

who being elected tried and sworn the truth to speak upon the issue joined, upon their Oath do say that Deft. is Guilty in manner and form as Plt. against him hath complained and they do assess Plt.'s damages by occasion thereof to three pounds, ten shillings current money besides his costs. Therefore it is considered by the Court that Plt. recover against Deft. his damages aforesaid in form aforesaid assessed and his costs by him about his suit in this behalf expended, and Deft. in mercy, &c.

p.   Loudoun County Court 11th of March 1762
571   - The Petition of AENEAS CAMPBELL, Gent. against JACOB READ is dismissed, being agreed by the parties
        - Upon Petition of AENEAS CAMPBELL, Gent., against JOHN PILES for a Debt due by Account, This day came Plt. in his proper person and Deft. having been duly summoned was solemnly called but came not. Therefore it is considered by the Court that Plt. recover against Deft. four pounds, two shillings and three pence half penny and his costs by him in this behalf expended
        - Upon Petition of AENEAS CAMPBELL, Gent., against THOMAS EATON for a Debt due by Account; This day came Plt. in his proper person and Deft. having been duly summoned was solemnly called but came not. Therefore it is considered by the Court that Plt. recover against Deft. three pounds and six pence half penny and his costs by him in this behalf expended
        - Upon Petition of AENEAS CAMPBELL, Gent. against WILLIAM ENNIS for a Debt due by Account, This day came Plt. in his proper person and Deft. having been duly summoned was solemnly called but came not; Therefore it is considered by the Court that Plt. recover against Deft. three pounds, ten shillings and ten pence half penny and his costs by him in this behalf expended
        - Upon Petition of AENEAS CAMPBELL, Gent., against JOHN WALTON for a Debt due by Account, This day came Plt. in his proper person and Deft. having been duly summoned was solemnly called but came not; Therefore it is considered by the Court that Plt. recover against Deft. three pounds and eight pence and his costs by him in this behalf expended
        - The Petition of AENEAS CAMPBELL, Gent. against GEORGE VANDI-VIER is dismissed, being agreed by the parties, and it is ordered that Deft. pay unto Plt. his costs
        - The Petition of AENEAS CAMPBELL, Gent., against WILLIAM THOMPSON is discontinued
        - Upon Petition of AENEAS CAMPBELL, Gent. against SAMUEL WILKS for a Debt due by Account, This day came Plt. in his proper person and Deft. having been duly summoned was solemnly called but came not; Therefore it is considered by the Court that Plt. recover against Deft. two pounds, six shillings and eight pence half penny and his costs by him in this behalf expended
        - Upon Petition of AENEAS CAMPBELL, Gent., against WILLIAM MOR-LAND for a Debt due by Account, This day came the parties by their Attornies who being fully heard, it is considered by the Court that Plt. recover against Deft. two pounds, nine shillings and two pence and his costs by him in this behalf expended
        - The Petition of AENEAS CAMPBELL, Gent., against JOHN CARGYLE is dismissed, being agreed by the parties
        - The Petition of WILLIAM ELLZEY against HENRY PARKER is dismissed,

being agreed by the parties

p.   Loudoun County Court 11th of March 1762
572   - ALEXANDER BROWN and COMPANY, Plts. agt. JOSIAS CLAPHAM,
       Deft.   In Case
This day came as well Plts. by FRANCIS DADE, their Attorney, as Deft. in his
proper person and Deft. relinquishing his former Plea saith that he cannot gainsay
the action of Plts. for fifteen pounds, six shillings and seven pence. Therefore it is
considered by the Court that Plts. recover against Deft. the fifteen pounds, six
shillings and seven pence and their costs by them in this behalf expended, and Deft. in
mercy, &c.
       - Ordered that the Sherif summon ANN GRIFFIN to appear here at next
Court to answwer an Information exhibited against her by CHARLES TYLER and
FRANCIS PEYTON, Gent., Churchwardens for the time being for the Parish of
Cameron for having a base born Child
       - Ordered that the Sherif summon ELIZABETH BLACK to appear here at
next Court to answer an Information exhibited against her by CHARLES TYLER
and FRANCIS PEYTON, Gent., Churchwardens for the time being for the Parish of
Cameron for having a base born Child
       - Upon Petition of WILLIAM DODD against JOHN WORMSLEY for a Debt
due by Account, This day came the parties by their Attornies who being fully heard,
it is considered by the Court that Plt. recover against Deft. one pound, ten shillings
and four pence half penny and his costs by him in this behalf expended
       - The Petition of PHILIP LANGFIT against SAMPSON TURLEY is continued
till next Court for award
       - The Petition of JAMES KENNERLY, Assignee of ELIZABETH VICK,
against BENJAMIN GRAYSON, Gent., is continued till next Court by consent of the
parties
       - The Petition of THOMPSON MASON, Esqr. against BENJAMIN MASON is
dismissed
       - WILLIAM DODD, agt. JAMES VESSELL,   On Petition
Ordered that JOHN MOSS and JAMES HAMILTON, Gent., do value the work
done by Deft. for Plt. and make a report thereof to the Court
       - The Petition of THOMAS PHILLIPS against JOSIAS CLAPHAM, Gent., is
continued till next Court at motion and costs of Plt.
       - Upon Petition of JACOB GARDNER against SAMUEL WINN for a Debt
due by Account; This day came the parties by their Attornies and being fully heard, it
is considered by the Court that Plt. recover against Deft. five hundred twenty pounds
of tobacco and his costs by him in this behalf expended

p.   Loudoun County Court 11th of March 1762
573   - The Petition of JOHN MEHERG against WILLIAM HUTCHISON is continued till next Court by consent of the parties
       - The Petition of SETH JOHNSON against THOMAS TRAMMELL is con-
tinued till next Court by consent of the parties
       - GEORGE HEADEN, Plt. against JOHN O'CAIN, Deft. In Debt
On motion of Plt.'s Attorney further time is allowed him to reply till next Court

- JOHN TRAMELL and SAMPSON TRAMELL, Exrs. & Legatees of the Last Will and Testament of JOHN TRAMELL, late of County of FAIRFAX, deced, Plts. agt. JOHN HOPKINS, Deft.   In Debt

On motion of Plts. by their Attorney, further time is allowed them to reply till next Court

- THOMAS HARRISON, JAMES NISBET, BENJAMIN GRAYSON and SPENCE GRAYSON, Exrs. &c. of the Last Will and Testament of BENJA-MIN GRAYSON, Gent., deced., Plts. agt. GEORGE HANCOCKE, Deft. In Case

Continued till next Court at motion and costs of Plts.

- THOMAS BULLITT, Plt. agt. CHARLES LEWIS, Deft.   In Case

Continued till next Court by consent of the parties

- Present AENEAS CAMPBELL, Gent.

- Aminidab Goodtitle, Lessee of JOHN WATSON, Plt. against LEWIS ELLZEY, Deft. In Ejectment for one messuage & one hundred fifty acres of land with the appurtenances lying & being in the Parish of Cameron & County of Loudoun

Continued till next Court at motion and costs of Plt.

-ARCHIBALD CAMPBELL, Clerk, Plt. against JOHN ANDREWS, other-wise called I JOHN ANDREWS, of Parish of Cameron and County of FAIR-FAX, Clerk, Deft.   In Debt

This day came the parties by their Attornies and Deft. relinquishing his former Plea saith he cannot gainsay Plt.'s action. Therefore it is considered by the Court that Plt. recover against Deft. one thousand nine hundred sixty pounds of crop tobacco, the Debt in the Declaration mentioned, and his costs by him about his suit in this behalf expended, and Deft. in mercy, &c., But this Judgment is to be discharged by paiment of nine hundred eighty pounds of tobacco together with Interest for the same to be computed after the rate of five per-

p.   Loudoun County Court 11th of March 1762
574   centum per annum from the nineteenth day of May 1755 till the time of paiment and the costs

- ALEXANDER FARROW, Plt. agt. RICHARD FREEMAN and ELIZA-BETH FREEMAN, Defts.   In Case

Continued till next Court at motion and costs of Plt.

- ANN VANDIVIER, Wife of GEORGE VANDIVIER, an Evidence for JOHN DAVIS and MARGARET his Wife, late MARGARET DAVIS, Admrx. of THOMAS DAVIS, the Elder, deced. against ELIZABETH DAVIS, Admrx. of THOMAS DAVIS the Younger, deced., having attended Court two daies, ordered that said JOHN and MARGARET pay her fifty pounds of tobacco for the same

- JOHN DAVIS and MARGARET his Wife, late MARGARET DAVIS, Admrx. of THOMAS DAVIS, the Elder, Plts. agt. ELIZABETH DAVIS, Admrx. of THOMAS DAVIS, the Younger, deced., Deft.   In Case

This day came the parties by their Attornies and thereupon came also a Jury to

wit;		
JOHN MINOR	BENJAMIN MASON	WILLIAM WINN
SAMUEL WINN	LEVEN POWELL	JOHN MUIR
MARK CHILTON	THOMAS MIDDLETON	CHARLES CHILTON
STIRMAN CHILTON	WILLIAM PEARL and	MICHAEL VAN BUSCARK

who being elected tried and sworn the truth to speak upon the issue joined, upon their Oath do say that Deft. is Not Guilty as in Pleading she hath alledged; Therefore it is considered by the Court that Plts. take nothing by their Bill but for their false clamour be in mercy, &c., and the Deft. go thereof without day and recover against Plts. her costs by her about her defence in this behalf expended

       - Absent. JAMES HAMILTON, Gent.

       - JAMES MACCUBBIN, Plt. agt. JOHN SHEPHERD, Deft.   In Debt
This day came the parties by their Attornies and thereupon came also a Jury to wit,

JOHN MOSS, JUNR.	ROBERT DOUGLASS	GRIFFIS MERRICK
FRANKLIN PERRY	WILLIAM DOUGLASS	JOHN SINCLAIR
JOHN LEWIS	WILLIAM TRAMEL	EDWARD HARDEN
JOSEPH MOXLEY	THOMAS SORRELL and	THOMAS LEWIS

who being elected tried and sworn the truth to speak upon the issue joined, upon their Oath do say that Deft. hath not paid to Plt. nine pounds, seven shillings and two pence current money, the Debt in the Declaration mentioned, in manner and formas Plt. against him hath complained and they do assess the

p.   Loudoun County Court 11th of March 1762
575   Plt.'s damages by occasion of the detention of said Debt to one penny current
       money besides his costs. Therefore it is considered by the Court that Plt. recover against Deft. his Debt aforesaid together with his damages aforesaid in form aforesaid assessed and his costs by him about his suit in this behalf expended, and Deft. in mercy, &c.

       - AENEAS CAMPBELL, Gent., Plt. agt. JOHN BISHOP, Deft.   In Case
This suit is dismissed being agreed by the parties

       - The Petition of JOSEPH STEPHENS against JOSEPH JANNEY is continued till next Court by consent of the parties

       - THOMAS LEWIS, an Evidence for JACOB GARDNER, against SAMUEL WINN having attended Court eleven daies, ordered that said JACOB pay him two hundred seventy five pounds of tobacc for the same

       - CHARLES CHILTON, an Evidence for JACOB GARDNER, against SAMUEL WINN, having attended Court eleven daies, ordered that said JACOB pay him two hundred seventy five pounds of tobacco for the same

       - MARK CHILTON, an Evidence for JACOB GARDNER, against SAMUEL WINN having attended Court twelve daies, ordered that said JACOB pay him three hundred pounds of tobacco for the same

       - JAMES LEITH, an Evidence for JACOB GARDNER, against SAMUEL WINN having attended Court three days, ordered said JACOB pay him seventy five pounds of tobacco for the same

       - WILLIAM WINN, an Evidence for SAMUEL WINN, at the suit of JACOB GARDNER, having attended Court five daies and for travelling eighteen miles from PRINCE WILLIAM County and returning twice, ordered that said SAMUEL pay him two hundred thirty three pounds of tobacco for the same

       - WILLIAM ATTERBERRY, an Evidence for SAMUEL WINN, at the suit of JACOB GARDNER having attended Court five days, ordered said SAMUEL pay him one hundred twenty five pounds of tobacco for the same

         - Ordered that the Court be adjourned till tomorrow morning eight o'clock

         - The Minutes of these Proceedings were signed "AENS. CAMPBELL "

p.   - At a Court continued and held for Loudoun County at the Courthouse on
576   Friday the Twelfth day of March one thousand seven hundred and sixty two,
      Before his Majesty's Justices of the Peace for the said County, to wit;
              JAMES HAMILTON   NICHOLAS MINOR &
              AENEAS CAMPBELL   GEORGE WEST, Gent.

      - The Petition of Messrs. ARMSTRONG and CRAWFORD against RICHARD
BUCKLEW is continued till next Court at motion and costs of Plts.
      - THOMAS HARRISON, JAMES NISBET, BENJAMIN GRAYSON and
      SPENCE GRAYSON, Exrs. of the Last Will and Testament of BENJAMIN
      GRAYSON, Gent., deced., Plts. agt. JOHN KING, Deft.   In Case
Continued till next Court at motion and costs of Plts.
      - WILLIAM GOSSETT, JUNR., Plt. agt. SAMUEL DAVIS, JUNR. Deft.
      In Trespass Assault and Battery
The Deft. being arrested and not appearing altho' solemnly called, on motion of Plt.
by HUGH WEST, his Attorney, it is ordered that unless Deft. shall appear here at
next Court and answer Plt.'s action, Judgment shall then be given for Plt. against
Deft. and SAMUEL DAVIS and JOHN DAVIS, who are returned Securities for his
appearance, for his damages and costs
              - Present. CHARLES TYLER, Gent.
      - ROBERT POPKINS, Plt. agt. JOHN PHILIPS, Deft.   In Case
The Deft being again returned not to be found, on motion of Plt.'s Attorney another
Plurius Capias is awarded him returnbale here at next Court
      - CRAVEN PEYTON, Plt. agt. JOHN PHILIPS, Deft.   In Case
Continued till next Court
      - FRANCIS HERONIMUS, Plt. agt. WILLIAM RUST, Deft.   In Trespass
This day came the parties by their Attornies and Deft. saving to himself all advan-
tages of Exceptions as well to Plt.'s Writ as to his Declaration, prays and has leave to
imparl till next Court and then to plead

p.   Loudoun County Court 12th of March 1762
577   - JOSIAS CLAPHAM, Gent. and SARAH his Wife, Admrx. of all and singular
      the goods and chattels, rights and credits which were of RODOLPHUS
      ELTINGEE, deceased, Plts. against JOHN WALTON, Deft.   In Debt
The Deft. being arrested and not appearing altho' solemnly called, on motion of Plts.
by HUGH WEST, their Attorney, it is ordered that unless Deft. shall appear here at
next Court and answer Plt.'s action, Judgment shall then be given for Plt. against
Deft. and MICHAEL VAN BUSCART and ROBERT POPKINS, who are returned
Securites for his appearance for his damages and costs
      - JAMES GOULDING, Plt. against BENJAMIN GRAYSON, Deft.
      In Trespass Assault and Battery and False Imprisonment
This day came the parties by their Attornies and Deft. saving to himself all advantages of Exceptions as well to Plt.'s Writ as to his Declaration, prays and has leave to
imparl till next Court and then to plead
      - SAMUEL EARLE, Plt. against WILLIAM FURR, Deft.   In Debt
The Deft. being arrested and not appearing altho' solemnly called, on motion of Plt.
by FRANCIS DADE, his Attorney, it is ordered that unless Deft. shall appear here at

next Court and answer Plt.'s action, Judgment shall then be given for Plt. against him and EDWARD GARRETT, who is returned Security for his appearance, for the Debt in the Declaration mentioned and costs

  - CRAVEN PEYTON, Plt. against JAMES DAVIS, Deft. In Case

The Deft. being returned not found, on motion of Plt. by HUGH WEST, his Attorney, an Alias Capias is awarded him returnable here at next Court

  - MARTIN ARMSTRONG, Plt. against ARCHIBALD CRAWFORD, Deft. In Covenant

Continued till next Court by consent of the parties

  - ARCHIBALD CRAWFORD, Plt. against MARTIN ARMSTRONG, Deft. In Case

Continued till next Court by consent of the parties

p. Loudoun County Court 12th of March 1762
578 - CRAVEN PEYTON, Plt. agt. THOMAS SORRELL, Deft. In Case

This suit is dismissed, being agreed by the parties

  - JOSEPH WILLIAMS, Plt. agt. WILLIAM HARRELL, Deft. In Case

This suit is discontinued, the Plt. not further prosecuting

  - WILLIAM HUTCHISON, Plt. agt. JOHN NEVILL, Deft. In Case

This day came the parties by their Attornies and Deft. saving to himself all advantages of Exceptions as well to Plt.'s Writ as to his Declaration, prays and has leave to imparl till next Court and then to plead

  - ROBERT HAMILTON, Plt. agt. JAMES VESSELLS, Deft.

  In Trespass Assault and Battery

This day came the parties by their Attornies and Deft. saving to himself all advantages of Exceptions as well to Plt.'s Writ as to his Declaration, prays and has leave to imparl till next Court and then to plead

  - JOHN EVINS, Plt. agt. DANIEL McGINNIS and JOHN BISHOP, Defts.

  In Debt

The Deft. JOHN BISHOP, appeared and being ruled to Special Bail and failing so to do, on motion of Plt. by his Attorney, Deft. is committed to the Common Goal of this County of Debtors and it is ordered that Judgment be entered for Plt. against Deft. for the Debt in the Declaration mentioned and costs unless Deft. shall give such Bail and plead to issue at the next Court. The Deft., DANIEL McGINNIS, being returned not to be found, an Alias Capias is awarded him returnable &c.

  - JAMES INGOE DOZER, Plt. agt. SAMUEL WINN, Deft. In Case

The Deft. being arrested and not appearing altho' solemnly called, on motion of Plt. by WILLIAM ELLZEY, his Attorney, it is ordered that unless Deft. shall appear here at next Court and answer Plt.'s action, Judgment shall then be given for Plt. against him and JOHN WINN, who is returned Security for his appearance, for his damages and costs

p. Loudoun County Court 12th of March 1762
579 - BENJAMIN EDWARDS, Plt. agt. JOHN OWSLEY, otherwise called I
  JOHN OWSLEY of County of Loudoun, Deft. In Debt

The Deft. being arrested and not appearing altho' solemnly called, on motion of Plt. by WILLIAM ELLZEY his Attorney, it is ordered that unless Deft. shall appear here at next Court and answer Plt.'s action, Judgment shall then be given for Plt. against him and ROBERT STEVENS, who is returned Security for his appearance, for the Debt in the Declaration mentioned and costs

- SAMUEL PHILLIPS, Plt. agt. EDWARD SAMS, Deft.   In Debt

The Deft. being returned not to be found, on motion of Plt. an Alias Capias is awarded him returnable here at next Court

- RICHARD ROGERS, Plt. agt. JOHN WALTON, Deft.   In Debt

The Deft. being arrested and not appearing altho' solemnly called, on motion of Plt. by his Attorney, it is ordered that unless Deft. shall appear here at next Court and answer Plt.'s action, Judgment shall then be given for Plt. against him and SAMUEL HARRIS, who is returned Security for his appearance, for the Debt in the Declaration mentioned and costs

- The Petition of MARTIN ARMSTRONG against WILLIAM HARRELL is discontinued

- The Petition of GEORGE ROSS against WILLIAM HARRELL is discontinued

- Ordered that DAVID SMITH be appointed CONSTABLE for this County

- CRAVEN PEYTON, Plt. agt. HENRY PICKERILL, Deft.
Upon an Attachment

This suit is dismissed being agreed by the parties

- Ordered that a Licence be granted to BENJAMIN EDWARDS to keep an ORDINARY at his House in LEESBURGH for one year from this time, he with Security having entered into Bond as the Law directs

- Upon Petition of STURMAN CHILTON against THOMAS PRITCHARD for a Debt due by Account, This day came the parties by their Attornies who being fully heard, it is considered by the Court that Plt. recover against Deft. two pounds, twelve shillings and one penny farthing and his costs by him in this behalf expended

- The Petition of WILLIAM OWSLEY against WILLIAM BURKLEY is discontinued

- The Petition of FRANCIS HERONIMUS against JOHN WALDEN is discontinued

p.   Loudoun County Court 12th of March 1762
580   - Upon Petition of WILLIAM DODD against JAMES GOULDING for a Debt
        due by Account, This day came Plt. by HUGH WEST, his Attorney, and Deft. having been duly summoned was solemnly called but came not; Therefore it is considered by the Court that Plt. recover against Deft. two pounds, eight shillings and ten pence, his Debt now proved due, and his costs by him in this behalf expended

- The Petition of JOHN OWSLEY, against WILLIAM CONNELL is continued till next Court at motion and costs of Plt.

- The Petition of JOHN POSEY against WILLIAM OWSLEY is continued till next Court at motion and costs of Plt.

- The Petition of DENNIS DALLIS against JONATHAN DAVIS is dismissed, being agreed by the parties

- Upon Petition of JACOB SHILLING against JAMES VESSELLS for a Debt due by Account, This day came the parties by their Attornies who being fully heard, it is considered by the Court that the Petition be dismissed and that Plt. pay unto Deft.

his costs
- The Petition of JAMES FOWLER against PHILIP FOUGHT is continued till next Court by consent of the parties
- Present. RICHARD COLEMAN & JOSIAS CLAPHAM, Gent.
- The Petition of JOHN CHAMP, JUNR. against WILLIAM HUTCHISON is continued till next Court by consent of the parties
- The Petition of BENJAMIN EDWARDS against JAMES LAYTON is discontinued
- Upon Petition of BENJAMIN EDWARDS against JAMES GOULDING for a Debt due by Account; This day came Plt. in his proper person and Deft. altho' solemnly called came not. Therefore it is considered by the Court that Plt. recover against Deft. two pounds, seven shillings and three pence, his Debt now proved due & his costs by him in this behalf expended
- Upon Petition of BENJAMIN EDWARDS against JOHN BISHOP for a Debt due by Account, This day came the parties in their proper persons and Deft. acknowledged Plt.'s demand for two pounds fourteen shillings and two pence half penny to be just; Therefore it is considered by the Court that Plt. recover against Deft. said two pounds, fourteen shillings and two pence half penny and his costs by him in this behalf expended
- Upon Petition of CRAVEN PEYTON against SHADRICK CHAVIS for a Debt due by Account, This day came Plt. by HUGH WEST, his Attorney, an Deft. having been duly summoned was solemnly called but came not; Therefore it is considered by the Court that Plt. recover against Deft. three pounds, twelve shillings and four pence, his Debt now proved due, and his costs by him in this behalf expended
- Upon Petition of CRAVEN PEYTON against SAMUEL PHILLIPS for a Debt due by Account, This day came Plt. by HUGH WEST, his Attorney and Deft. having been duly summoned was

p.   Loudoun County Orders 12th of March 1762
581   solemnly called but came not. Therefore it is considered by the Court that Plt.
        recover against Deft. one pound, eight shillings and an half penny, his Debt now
proved dur and his costs by him in this behalf expended
- The Petition of CRAVEN PEYTON against BENJAMIN BAUZELL is dismissed, being agreed by the parties
- Upon Petition of CRAVEN PEYTON against JAMES FORGESON for a Debt due by Account, This day came Plt. by HUGH WEST, his Attorney, and Deft. having been duly summoned was solemnly called but came not, Therefore it is considered by the Court that Plt. recover against Deft. two pounds, six shillings and five pence farthing, his Debt due as aforesaid, and his costs by him in this behalf expended
- Absent JAMES HAMILTON, AENEAS CAMPBELL &
                NICHOLAS MINOR, Gent.
- Indentures of Lease and Release between BENJAMIN · SHRIEVE and ANN his Wife of one part and JOHN BERKTLEY of the other part were acknowledged by said BENJAMIN and ANN, she having been first privily examined as the Law directs, and the Receipt thereon endorsed was acknowledged by said BENJAMIN and together with the Indentures, ordered to be recorded

- FRANCIS PEYTON, Gent., Plt. agt. THOMAS DONOHOE, Deft. In Case
This suit is dismissed being agreed by the parties
- CRAVEN PEYTON, Plt. agt. THOMAS LIDDLE, Deft.
Upon an Attachment
Continued till next Court for Garnishee to declare
- Ordered that the Court be adjourned till the second Tuesday in April next
- The Minutes of these Proceedings were signed
" RICHD: COLEMAN "

p. 582

-At a Court held at the Courthouse of Loudoun County on Tuesday the Twenty third day of March 1762; for the Examination of WILLIAM McDANIELL on Suspicion of his being Guilty of Feloniously Forging of five Treasurer Notes, two of the value of ten shillings each and three of the value of five shillings each   Present

JAMES HAMILTON	GEORGE WEST	
AENEAS CAMPBELL	FRANCIS PEYTON	&
NICHOLAS MINOR	JAMES LANE,	Gent.

The said WILLIAM McDANIELL was set to the Bar and it being demanded of him whether he was Guilty of the Felony aforesaid or not, he said he was not thereof Guilty and thereupon HENRY MOORE, DANIEL DESKINS, BURKETT JETT, CHARLES ESKRIDGE, JAMES WHALEY JOHN MILLER, WILLIAM SEARS and JOHN GODDARD were sworn & examined as witnesses against him and he heard in his own defence. On Consideratiion whereof it is the opinion of the Court that said WILLIAM is Guilty of a Misdemeanor. Whereupon said WILLIAM submitted himself to the Judgment of the Justices now sitting to inflict on him any Punishment that the Justices should think proper. Therefore it is considered by the Court that he receive at the Public Whiping Post twenty lashes on his bare back well laid on & it is commanded the Sherif that he cause immediate execution thereof to be done, And nothing further appearing against him, it is ordered that he be then discharged out of custody.
The Minutes of these Proceedings were signed
" JAS: HAMILTON "

(Loudoun County Order Book, 1757-1762 will continue in another book, beginning on page 582 with a new Commission of the Peace sworn for Loudoun County, the ceremony held at the Court House on Tuesday the Eleventh day of May 1762).

ABBETT / ABIT
  Ann Wife of James, an Exr. of Mary Jennings
     16,
  James 5, 8, 9, 12, 16. 21, 28, 65,
ADAM.
  Andrew 2, 14, 15, 28, 31, 38, 39, 44, 45, 48,
     49, 60, 65, 69, 72, 78, 89, 90,
  Andrew Mercht. 70,
  Robert 15, 16, 88,
  Robert Gent. 10, 88,
ADAMS.
  Daniel 13,
  Elizabeth Wife of Gabriel deced. 64,
  Gabriel deced., (Will proved -2), 64, (Inv.
     retd. -93),
  William Exr. of Gabriel, deced. 2, 64,
ADDAMS.
  Sill 72,
ALEXANDER.
  Gerard Gent. 20,
ALLAN.
  George 65,
  John 65,
  William 65, 82-84,
  William Esqr. 3,
ALLERSON.
  Bryan 27, 36, 41,
ANDERSON.
  John 48, 67, 70, 73, 89,
ANDREWS.
  John Clerk of Fairfax Co. 18, 42, 96,
ANSLEY.
  Henry deced. 47, 52, 91,
  Mary 36,
  Mary Admrx. of Henry, deced. 47, (now Wife
     of Jonathan Monkhouse -91),
ARMSTRONG.
  Martin 49, 78, 82, 93, 99, 100,
ARMSTRONG & CRAWFORD
  Messrs. 98,
ARNETT.
  Alexander 86,
ARTIST.
  Tarvin 85,
ASHBY's Gap
  13,
ASHTON.
  Henry deced. 9, 11,
  Janes Admrx. of Henry deced. 9, 11,
ATTERBERRY.
  William 97,
AUSTINN.
  Isaac 87,
AWBREY.
  Elizabeth Widow & Relict of Henry 23,
  Henry deced. 23,

AWBREY (contd.)
  Thomas 20, 32, 40, 45, 52, 65, 69, 78, 84, 92,
  Thomas Admr. of Walter English, deced. 7,
     47, 67,

BAKER.
  William 5, 34, 38, 39, 43, 49, 61, 68, 77, 82,
BALDWIN.
  Francis 23, 37,
BALL.
  Farlan 55,
  John 64, 65, 91,
BALLENGER.
  Francis 58, 60, 68, 77,
BARKLEY.
  William 79,
BARNES.
  Abraham 14, 20, 54,
BARTLESON.
  Richard 31, 81, 82,
BAUZELL.
  Benjamin 101,
BAYLIS.
  William 6,
BEASON.
  Jacob 14,
BEAVIS.
  William 88,
BERKLEY.
  Benjamin 38, 39, 41,
  Burgess deced. 17, 49, 67,
  Stacey Admr. of Burgess, now Wife of Benjamin
     Grayson 17, 49, 67,
  William 17, 28, 49, 67,
BERKTLEY
  John 101,
BERRY.
  Rebecca Wife of Wm. 21, 41,
  William 21, 28, 41, 43,
BINNS.
  Charles 1, 5, 6, 64,
  Charles Clerk of Court 65,
  Charles Gent. 80,
BISHOP.
  John 14, 30, 55, 97, 99, 101,
  Samuel 16,
BLACK.
  Elizabeth 95,
  Hugh 9, (apptd. Constable -25), 30, 31, 53,
  William 14, 64, 65,
BLACKBURN.
  Thomas 35,
BLINCOE.
  Thomas Carpenter 72,
BOGGESS.
  Henry Junr. 47, 48,

JOHNSON.
  Francis 20,
  John 53,
  Seth 84, 95,
JOHNSTON.
  George Gent. 29, 40,
JOICE.
  James 41,
JONES.
  Daniel 29,
  Joseph 48, 54,
  Thomas 15, 49,
  William 25, 79,
JORDAN.
  Mary 51, 69,
JUSTICES (first appearance at Court)
  CAMPBELL, Aeneas 6,
  CLAPHAM, Josias 7,
  COLEMAN. Richard 10,
  GRAYSON, Benjamin 1,
  HAMILTON, James 1,
  LANE, James 6,
  MINOR. Nicholas 35,
  MUCKLEHANEY, John 1,
  PEYTON, Francis 1,
  TURNER, Fielding 1,
  TYLER, Charles 1,
  WEST, George 1,

KANNIDAY.
  James (Trial on Suspicion of Stealing -9), 12,
KEEN.
  Richard 30, 31, 62, 82,
KELLEY.
  Thomas 7, 17, 39, 41, 42, 46, 67, 80,
KENNERLY
  James 32, 39, 95,
KERRIGIN
  Hugh 64, 65,
KILLIHAM
  John 53, 84,
KING.
  John 9, 11, 12, 20, 48, 50, 66, 98,
  John Exr. of Richard Osborn, deced. 88,
KIRK.
  William (Mill of -3),
KIRKPATRICK.
  John 76,

LACKEY.
  John 13, 48, 67,
LADD.
  Benjamin 70,
LAMB.
  Thomas Quaker 62, 63,

LAMBERT.
  John 72,
LANE.
  James Churchwarden of Cameron Parish 15,
      47, 70,
  James Gent. 1, 30, 76,
  James Justice 6,
  James Junr. 2, 24, (Captain in Militia 27),
  William Carr 63, 76,
LANGFIT.
  Philip 29, 40, 95,
LASSWELL.
  Jacob exempt from Levies & Poll Tax 53,
LAY.
  Immanuel 87,
  Sylvanus 87,
LAYTON.
  James 101,
  James Admr. of Wm. 58, 69,
  William deced. 58, 69,
LEATHERMAN.
  Michael 35,
LEE
  Francis Lightfoot Gent. 66,
  Francis Lightfoot first Justice in Commission
      of the Peace 10,
LEESBURGH.
  Town of 3,
LEITH.
  James 13, 18, 21, 24, 30, 31, 35, 38, 42, 44,
      47, 49, 58, 65, 72, 75, 97,
LEWELLEN./ LEWELLING
  Shadrick 51,
  Thomas 3, 9, 27, 38, 88,
LEWIS.
  Charles 5, 42, 58, 68, 96,
  Elizabeth 38, 50, 68, 93,
  Elizabeth Admrx. of Stephen, deced. now Wife
      of Wm. Douglas 45; 50,
  Elizabeth married Wm. Douglas 17, 45, 68,
  John 9, 12, (apptd. Constable) 25, 30, 31, 89,
      92, 97,
  Levy 9, 31,
  Sarah Widow & Relict of Thomas, deced. 17,
      50, 68,
  Stephen deced. 45,
  Thomas 2, 8, 9, 12, 13, 37-39, 43, 49, 54, 74,
      75, 79, 86, 92, 97,
  Thomas deced. 17, 50, 68,
  Vincent 63, 76,
  William 38,
LIDDLE.
  Thomas 73, 102.
LINK.
  Andrew 34, 68,

OSBORN.
  John 3, 35,
  Nicholas 4, 26,
  Nicholas Junr. 4,
  Richard deced. 88,
OSGOODTHARP
  Richard 88,
OWSLEY.
  John 9, 19, 64, 67, 71, 81, 83-86, 99, 100,
  Newdigate 7, 8, 10,
  Thomas 7, 9, 13, 24, 27, 63, 83, 84,
  William 7, 16, 26, 27, 30, 31, 54, 58, 77, 85,
      100,
  William of Fairfax Co. 52,

PAGAN.
  John 49,
PALMER.
  Daniel 46, 65,
  John 46, 65.
  John Junr. 46,
  Thomas 46, 47, 65,
PARKER.
  Anthony 82,
  Henry 85, 94,
PATTERSON.
  Fleming 73, 76, 78, 89, 90,
  John 38, 74,
  John Gent. 39, 40,
  Samuel 15, 64, 77,
PEAKE.
  John 1, 2,
PEARL.
  William 7, 59, 77, 96, -
PEARSON.
  Milkey Wife of Simon 19, 50, 52, 67, 68,
  Simon 19, 50, 52, 67, 68,
PERFECT.
  Christopher 7, 9, 13, 27, 34, (a Constable -90),
PERRY.
  Franklin 11, 14, 31, 47, 54, 67, 97,
PEYTON.
  Craven 7, 13, 14, 32, 36, 45, 48, 60, 65, 68,
      70, 71, 73, 76, 77, 82, 84-86, 89,
      98-102.
  Craven Mercht. Son in Law of Wm. West 34,
  Craven sworn Under Sheriff -50,
  Francis 30, 64,
  Francis Churchwarden Cameron Parish 12,
      13, 48, 56, 66, 95,
  Francis Gent. 24, 46, 52, 102.
  Francis Justice 1, 82,
  Henry 71, 78,
  Henry Gent. 18, 42, 69, 89, 91,
  John Gdn. of Robert 47,
  Robert an Infant under age 21; 47,

PFHAW / PHAW.
  Jacob 13, 41.
PHILLIPS.
  Ann Widow & Relict of John, deced. 23,
  Ann Wife of Thomas 37,
  Edmon 26,
  James Quaker 86,
  Jean Wife of Thomas 86,
  Jenkins 56,
  John 40, 45, 60, 65, 68, 77, 81, 98,
  John deced. 23,
  Philip 23,
  Samuel 22, 100, 101,
  Thomas 15, 37, 49, 55, 56, 60, 64, 65, 84, 86,
      95,
  Thomas Gdn. of Rebecca Eades 67,
PHILLIS.
  Joseph 27,
PICKREL(L)
  Henry 29, 90, 100,
PILES.
  John 1, 94,
  Richard 1,
PINKSTEAD.
  Christian 82,
PLUMMER.
  Ellen Wife of Thomas 26,
  Thomas 26,
POLLARD.
  Joseph 57,
POLLEN.
  Henry 75,
PONEL.
  Sarah 9,
POOLE.
  Benjamin 69,
POPKINS.
  John 30, 32,
  Robert 3, 32, 45, 65, 89, 92, 98,
POSEY.
  John 85, 100,
POTTS.
  Jonas 2,
  Jonas Blacksmith 59,
  Jonas Farmer 59,
  Mary Wife of Jonas 2,
  Mary Wife of Jonas Blacksmith 59,
POULTNEY.
  Elioner an Exr. of John deced. 14,
  John deced. 12, 14,
POWELL.
  Levin 19, 42, 71, 91-93, 96,
  Micajah (Ord. Lic.-89),
POWER.
  Joseph 67,

PRESTON.
  Isaac 6,
PRICE.
  Evan Gent. 26,
  John 1,
PRITCHARD.
  Rachel Wife of Thomas 26, 74, 80,
  Thomas 12, 15, 21, 26, 38, 39, 68, 71, 72,
      74, 80, 82, 85, 89, 100,
PROCTER.
  John a Mulatto base born Child bound out 80,
PYBURN.
  Thomas 49,
PYLES.
  John 17, 56, 85,

QUEEN.
  John 36,

RATCLIFF.
  John deced. 20,
  Susanna Admrx. of John, deced. 20,
RAWDERY.
  John an Orphan bound out 91,
REED / READ.
  Jacob 86, 87, 89, 94,
REMEY.
  Jacob 63,
  Jacob Junr. 36,
RICE.
  Patrick 8,
RICHARDS.
  John 52, 70,
RICHARDSON.
  Aaron 25, 73,
RILEY.
  John 51,
RIVERS:
  Potowmack 4, 26,
ROADS.
  Leesburg to Alexandria 80,
  Leesburg to Goose Creek 81,
  Mountain 14, 24. 26,
  Thomas Stump's Landing to Leesburg 27,
ROBERTS.
  Agnes Wife of Joseph 79,
  Ann Wife of Richard 79,
  Joseph 79,
  Joseph Son of Richard 62,
  Owen 7, 30, 31, 63, 65, 78, 90,
  Richard 3, 62, 72, 79,
ROBINSON.
  John 41,
RODEN.
  Thomas 54, 74,

RODGERS.
  James 58,
  Thomas 89,
ROGERS.
  James 19, 26, 76, 92, 93,
  Richard 100,
  Thomas 60, 73,
ROSE.
  Francis 85,
ROSS.
  David 15, 58,
  George 100,
  Hector 46, 67, ,
  Hector Gent. 10,
  James 37,
  William 2, 7-9, 12, 21, 28, 58, 69, 71, 79, 81,
      89,
  William Admr. of Thomas Evans, deced. 28,
RUNS:
  Broad 56, 57,
  Sugar Land 56,
  Tuscorora 81,
RUSSELL.
  Anthony 5, 77, 92,
  Anthony Gent. 5, 36, 40-42, 85,
RUST.
  William 78, 98,

SAMS.
  Edward 100,
SANDFORD.
  Robert 38, 39, 57, 75,
  Robert Junr. 47,
SANDERS.
  James 63,
SANGSTER.
  George 53,
SASSER.
  John 15, 30, 31, 62, 88,
SAUNDERS,
  James 43, 59,
  William 7, 47, 67, 88,
SCHOOLEY.
  Samuel 40,
SCOTT.
  Robert 6, 7,
SCRIEVE.
  Joseph 86,
SEALE.
  Anthony 46,
SEARS.
  William 102.
SEBASTIAN.
  Benjamin 4, 17, 22, 26, 29, 30, 40, 65,
  Benjamin Attorney 40, 50, 58, 73, 81, 82, 88,
  Benjamin Junr. 21, 24,

WEST.
  Catharine Wife of John, Gent. 26,
  Charles sworn Under Sheriff -50,
  George 20,
  George Gent. 1, 12, 13,
  George Gent. County Surveyor 28,
  George Justice 1,
  George Junr. 2,
  Hugh 2, 5. 18, 20, 30, 44, 69, 73, 80, 91, 92,
  Hugh Attorney 3, 4, 6, 8, 16, 17, 28, 29, 31,
      32, 36, 37, 40, 45, 47, 66, 67, 71, 73,
      74, 78, 81, 82, 84-86, 90, 92, 98-101,
  Hugh Deputy Attorney 65,
  Hugh Gent. 33, 54, 57, 79,
  John Gent. 26, 40,
  Joseph 28, 36, 37, 54, 58, 66,
  William 29, 60, 82,
  William Esqr. (apptd. Sheriff -33), 65, 71, 79,
  William Gent. 1, 25, 34, 57,
  William Junr. 33, (apptd. Under Sheriff -34),
      40, 43, 50, 59, 76,
WHALEY.
  James 30, 102.
WHITE.
  Richard 62,
WILDMAN.
  Jacob Quaker 2,
  William 22, 69,
  William Quaker 62, 63,
WILKS.
  Francis 4, 8, 26, 29,
  John 4, 91,
  Levi 53,
  Martha Wife of Francis 26,
  Samuel 62, 69, 94,
WILLIAMS.
  Edward 87,
  Evan 35,
  Joseph 99,
  Notley 86,
  Thomas 59, 79,
  Walter 59, 63,
WILLIAMSON.
  James 1,
  Nathan 15,
WILLIS.
  John 54,
WILLSON.
  James 60, 73, 89,
  John of Province of Maryland 26,
  Peter 84,
WINN.
  John 8, 9, 12, 20, 30, 72, 81, 82, 99,
  Minor 81, 91,
  Samuel 19, 54, 74, 75, 84, 92, 93, 95-97, 99,
  William 81, 82, 93, 96, 97,

WINSALL.
  Adam 37,
WINSOR.
  Mary 13, 56,
WINTNALE.
  John Martin 72, 75,
WISHEART.
  Henry 18, 41, 52, 63, 69, 78,
WOLLARD.
  William 8, 9, 12, 14, 21, 57,
WOOD.
  Robert 13, 14, 35, 36, 53, 71, 80, 89, 92,
WORMSLEY.
  John 6, 26, 30, 41, 76, 95,
WORTHINGTON.
  Robert 22,
WREN.
  Bernard 39,
  Catharine Wife of Bernard 39,
  Nicholas 66,
WRIGHT.
  Isaac Simpson 89,

YATES.
  Alice an Exr. of Joseph deced. 62,
  Joseph a Quaker 3, 16,
  Joseph deced. (Will proved -62), 63,
YELDALL.
  Francis 4,
  Robert 26,
YELDING.
  Robert 35,
YOUNG.
  Alexander & Co. 18,
  Bernard 3,
YOUNT.
  John 53,

Heritage Books by Ruth and Sam Sparacio

Essex County, Virginia Will Abstracts, 1743–1744

Essex County, Virginia Will Abstracts, 1745–1748

Essex County, Virginia Will Abstracts, 1748–1750

Fairfax County, Virginia Deed Abstracts, 1799–1800 and 1803–1804

Fairfax County, Virginia Deed Abstracts, 1804–1805

Fairfax County, Virginia Deed Book, 1795–1796

Fairfax County, Virginia Deed Book, 1796–1797

Fairfax County, Virginia Deed Abstracts, 1761–1768

Fairfax County, Virginia Deed Abstracts, 1772–1774

Fairfax County, Virginia Deed Book Abstracts, 1742–1750

Fairfax County, Virginia Deed Book Abstracts, 1750–1761

Fairfax County, Virginia Deed Book Abstracts, 1774–1777

Fairfax County, Virginia Deed Book Abstracts, 1784–1785

Fairfax County, Virginia Deed Book Abstracts, 1788–1789

Fairfax County, Virginia Deed Book Abstracts, 1789–1791

Fairfax County, Virginia Deed Book Abstracts, 1791–1792

Fairfax County, Virginia Deed Book Abstracts, 1792–1793

Fairfax County, Virginia Deed Book Abstracts, 1793–1795

Fairfax County, Virginia Deed Book Abstracts, 1796

Fairfax County, Virginia Deed Book Abstracts, 1797–1798

Fairfax County, Virginia Deed Book Abstracts, 1799

Fairfax County, Virginia Deed Book Abstracts, 1783–1784

Fairfax County, Virginia Deed Book Abstracts, 1785–1788

Fairfax County, Virginia Deed Book, 1798–1799

Fairfax County, Virginia Indexes of Missing Deed Books, 1750–1770

*Fairfax County, Virginia Index and References to
Missing Deed Book N, 1778–1783*

Fairfax County, Virginia Land Causes, 1788–1824

Fairfax County, Virginia Land Records of Long Standing, 1742–1770

Fairfax County, Virginia Order Book Abstracts, 1768–1769

Fairfax County, Virginia Order Book Abstracts, 1769–1770

Fairfax County, Virginia Will Book Abstracts, 1742–1745

Fairfax County, Virginia Will Book Abstracts, 1745–1748

Fairfax County, Virginia Will Book Abstracts, 1767–1783

Fairfax County, Virginia Will Book Abstracts, 1784–1791

Fairfax County, Virginia Will Book Abstracts, 1791–1794

Fairfax County, Virginia Will Book Abstracts, 1794–1798

Fairfax County, Virginia Will Book Abstracts, 1798–1801

Fauquier County, Virginia Land Tax Book, 1783–1787

Fauquier County, Virginia Land Tax Book, 1787–1791

Fauquier County, Virginia Minute Book Abstracts, 1759–1761

Fauquier County, Virginia Minute Book Abstracts, 1761–1762

Fauquier County, Virginia Minute Book Abstracts, 1762–1763

Fauquier County, Virginia Minute Book Abstracts, 1763–1764

Fauquier County, Virginia Minute Book Abstracts, 1764–1766

Fauquier County, Virginia Minute Book Abstracts, 1766–1767

Fauquier County, Virginia Minute Book Abstracts, 1767–1769

Fauquier County, Virginia Minute Book Abstracts, 1769–1771

Fauquier County, Virginia Minute Book Abstracts, 1771–1772

Fauquier County, Virginia Minute Book Abstracts, 1772–1773

Fauquier County, Virginia Minute Book Abstracts, 1773–1775

Fauquier County, Virginia Minute Book Abstracts, 1775–1779

Fauquier County, Virginia Minute Book Abstracts, 1779–1782

Fauquier County, Virginia Minute Book Abstracts, 1782–1783

Fauquier County, Virginia Minute Book Abstracts, 1783–1784

Fauquier County, Virginia Minute Book Abstracts, 1784–1785

Fauquier County, Virginia Minute Book Abstracts, 1785–1786

Fauquier County, Virginia Minute Book Abstracts, 1786–1787

Fauquier County, Virginia Minute Book Abstracts, 1787

Fauquier County, Virginia Minute Book Abstracts, 1787–1788

Fauquier County, Virginia Minute Book Abstracts, 1788–1789

Fauquier County, Virginia Minute Book Abstracts, 1789–1790

Fredericksburg City, Virginia Deed Book, 1782–1787

Fredericksburg City, Virginia Deed Book, 1787–1794

Fredericksburg City, Virginia Deed Book, 1794–1804

Hanover County, Virginia Land Tax Book, 1782–1788

Hanover County, Virginia Land Tax Book, 1789–1793

Hanover County, Virginia Land Tax Book, 1793–1796

King George County, Virginia Deed Book Abstracts, 1721–1735

King George County, Virginia Deed Book Abstracts, 1735–1752

King George County, Virginia Deed Book Abstracts, 1753–1773

King George County, Virginia Deed Book Abstracts, 1773–1783

King George County, Virginia Deed Book Abstracts, 1787–1790

King George County, Virginia Deed Book Abstracts, 1773–1783

King George County, Virginia Deed Book Abstracts, 1780–1787

King George County, Virginia Deed Book Abstracts, 1792–1794

King George County, Virginia Inventories, 1745–1765

King George County, Virginia Order Book Abstracts, 1721–1723

King George County, Virginia Order Book Abstracts, 1725–1728

King George County, Virginia Will Book Abstracts, 1752–1780

King William County, Virginia Record Book, 1702–1705

King William County, Virginia Record Book, 1705–1721

King William County, Virginia Record Book, 1722 and 1785–1786

Lancaster County, Virginia Deed and Will Book, 1652–1657

Lancaster County, Virginia Deed and Will Book, 1654–1661

*Lancaster County, Virginia Deed and Will Book, 1661–1702
(1661–1666 and 1699–1702)*

Lancaster County, Virginia Deed Book Abstracts, 1701–1706

Lancaster County, Virginia Deed Book, 1706–1710

Lancaster County, Virginia Deed Book, 1710–1714

Lancaster County, Virginia Order Book Abstracts, 1656–1661

Lancaster County, Virginia Order Book Abstracts, 1662–1666

Lancaster County, Virginia Order Book Abstracts, 1666–1669

Lancaster County, Virginia Order Book Abstracts, 1670–1674

Lancaster County, Virginia Order Book Abstracts, 1674–1678

Lancaster County, Virginia Order Book Abstracts, 1678–1681

Lancaster County, Virginia Order Book Abstracts, 1682–1687

Lancaster County, Virginia Order Book Abstracts, 1691–1695

Lancaster County, Virginia Order Book Abstracts, 1729–1732

Lancaster County, Virginia Order Book Abstracts, 1736–1739

Lancaster County, Virginia Order Book Abstracts, 1739–1742

Lancaster County, Virginia Order Book, 1687–1691

Lancaster County, Virginia Order Book, 1691–1695

Lancaster County, Virginia Order Book, 1695–1699

Lancaster County, Virginia Order Book, 1699–1701

Lancaster County, Virginia Order Book, 1701–1703

Lancaster County, Virginia Order Book, 1703–1706

Lancaster County, Virginia Order Book, 1732–1736

Lancaster County, Virginia Will Book, 1675–1689

Lancaster County, Virginia Will Book, 1690–1709

Loudoun County, Virginia Deed Book Abstracts, 1757–1762

Loudoun County, Virginia Deed Book Abstracts, 1762–1765

Loudoun County, Virginia Deed Book Abstracts, 1770–1772

Loudoun County, Virginia Deed Book Abstracts, 1771–1773

Stafford County, Virginia Will Book, 1729–1748

Stafford County, Virginia Will Book, 1748–1767

Westmoreland County, Virginia Deed and Will Abstracts, 1723–1726

Westmoreland County, Virginia Deed and Will Abstracts, 1726–1729

Westmoreland County, Virginia Deed and Will Abstracts, 1729–1732

Westmoreland County, Virginia Deed and Will Abstracts, 1732–1734

Westmoreland County, Virginia Deed and Will Abstracts, 1734–1736

Westmoreland County, Virginia Deed and Will Abstracts, 1736–1740

Westmoreland County, Virginia Deed and Will Abstracts, 1740–1742

Westmoreland County, Virginia Deed and Will Abstracts, 1742–1745

Westmoreland County, Virginia Deed and Will Abstracts, 1745–1747

Westmoreland County, Virginia Deed and Will Abstracts, 1747–1748

Westmoreland County, Virginia Deed and Will Abstracts, 1749–1751

Westmoreland County, Virginia Deed and Will Abstracts, 1751–1754

Westmoreland County, Virginia Deed and Will Abstracts, 1754–1756

Westmoreland County, Virginia Order Book, 1705–1707

Westmoreland County, Virginia Order Book, 1707–1709

Westmoreland County, Virginia Order Book, 1709–1712

Westmoreland County, Virginia Order Book, 1712–1714

Westmoreland County, Virginia Order Book, 1714–1716

Westmoreland County, Virginia Order Book, 1716–1718

Westmoreland County, Virginia Order Book, 1718–1721

www.ingramcontent.com/pod-product-compliance
Lightning Source LLC
Chambersburg PA
CBHW080336270326
41927CB00014B/3242